THE DRAGONS WHO ROARED

THE DRAGONS WHO ROARED

The Welsh Secondary Schools Tour of South Africa 1956

by Alan Evans

DAFFODIL PUBLISHING

First impression 2006

ISBN-10 0 9553274 0 7
ISBN-13 9780955327407

Printed in Wales at Gomer Press,
Llandysul, Ceredigion.

Contents

FOREWORD

It is a singular honour for me to write this Foreword in celebration of the fiftieth anniversary of the Welsh Secondary Schools' history making tour to South Africa in 1956.

A South African High Schools' side had toured Wales in the previous year, and, although I was to make my own international debut at schools' level in 1955, I missed by a couple of months the under-18 age limit game that Wales would play against the South Africans at Rodney Parade, Newport. This was to be one of the defining moments in the history of Welsh rugby, for it acted as the catalyst for the subsequent return tour by Wales to South Africa a year later and the first touring side at any age level to travel to the southern hemisphere. The 'Young Dragons' were created, and the format of Welsh rugby at national level would never be the same again.

All Welsh Secondary Schools' sides were full of accomplished and talented players, but the 'Class of 56' was an exceptional one and contained many who were to weave their way in and out of my life, both on and off the field, over the next fifty years.

Rhys Thomas, Alan Rees and Allan Williams were, of course, with me in the 'Class of 55'; in 1962 I was in the Wales senior side with Alan Rees and, three years later, with Clive Rowlands; and Rhys Thomas and I were to join up as National Servicemen and 'square bash' together in the Welch Regiment.

After National Service I worked for a time in Swansea and enjoyed sharing digs in Town Hill with fellow Scarlet, John Elgar Williams, but soon moved on to play with Jack Davies, a life-long friend, captain David Walkey, Graham Davies and Richie Griffiths for Cardiff.

Not all of the Young Dragons were to move on through the ranks of Welsh rugby. Indeed, some were to emigrate, to England and beyond, but hardly one of those who has remained has not crossed my path in rugby or in life, whether on the field of play, or in action or across some committee room in a rugby discussion. I eventually met Brian Skirrow as a working colleague in the 1990s at the International Rugby Board where he managed our Rugby World Cup tournament administration, whilst Clive Rowlands and myself seem to have been journeying through life and rugby for almost half-a-century, more as brothers than as brothers in arms, from Stradey Park to the 'Big Five' and on to the WRU presidency itself. Even our daughters were born in the same hospital bed, albeit not at the same time!

The sadness of any reunion is always for the absent friends, for Ned Gribble, Rowley Jones, the other officials who led Welsh rugby in its giant step forward, and more especially for the Young Dragons who have gone on to play in fairer realms above.

Yes, there will be sadness at the Reunion Dinner on 21 July 2006, but it will be part of the joy of remembrance and reunion for those rugby pioneers and history makers to whom those of us who have followed are truly indebted.

Thank you, 'Class of 56'.

Keith Rowlands
President, Welsh Rugby Union

INTRODUCTION

By David Walkey

Captain, The Young Dragons

Today is the era of professional rugby and there are regular Six Nations' tournaments and World Cups at 19 and 21 years of age and even the local high school XV may make tours to the southern hemisphere. It is difficult, therefore, to appreciate the full significance and magnitude of the decision in 1956 to take the Welsh Secondary Schools team to play a full tour of South Africa. It was the first ever tour to the southern hemisphere by any Welsh rugby team and for the 28 players involved and the six teachers who made up the management team it was to be an unforgettable experience and probably the most momentous two months of their lives. The team, most of whom had been born in 1937 and 1938, could remember childhood during the war years, and the austerity of post- war Britain. Many of us would have been fortunate to enjoy a week's holiday at Tenby or crossed the channel on a Campbell's paddle steamer to Weston-super-Mare. Cheap holiday flights to Spain or Florida were not even dreamt about. So a month's tour of South Africa, from Cape Town to the Rand, playing rugby against the legendary Springboks, was the ultimate experience any young rugby player could dream of.

For several of us, the prospect of the tour started in the 1954-55 season, when a strong Eastern Transvaal Schools XV toured Wales. It was suggested that a return visit should be made to South Africa the following year. I was selected to play for Monmouthshire against the touring team at Abertillery on 5 February 1955, but near-disaster had struck me early in the previous November when my left fibula was cracked in a school practice game. Fortunately luck was with me, and I played at Abertillery with a heavily strapped ankle on a very soft pitch and came through unscathed. After this match, I was more determined than ever to make any touring side, and shortly after the South African visit to Wales, it was officially confirmed that a WSSRU side would visit South Africa in the summer of 1956.

As with many things in life, luck would determine who would be eligible to make the trip – the luck of being the right age at the right time! A few players, including myself, were young enough to stay on at school for an extra year in the sixth form. For me this worked well, as I had passed two A levels in the summer of 1955 and was therefore able to spend the next academic year re-sitting one A level, but mainly concentrating on rugby and reaching a peak of fitness I had never previously attained. My selection for the tour was also aided at the beginning of the 1955-1956 season by the transfer of two international front row forwards, Neville Johnson and David 'Dai Fat' Williams, from New Tredegar Technical School to Bassaleg Grammar School. This resulted in our school team having a very strong pack, capable of dominating every other school team we played, and allowing Neville and myself to impress the selectors on numerous occasions. We were both eventually selected, but unfortunately David missed out.

Our 1956 domestic international season was far from outstanding. We narrowly lost to a strong Yorkshire Schools team at Rodney Parade and then only just managed to beat France at Cardiff Arms Park. The great consolation for me personally was that I had been awarded the captaincy for the French game and also the final game against England at Gloucester in late April. Unfortunately, we also lost the England game by a point. Since the players who had played in these three matches would inevitably form the core of the team to play in South Africa, this certainly was not an auspicious prelude to the tour, and must have given the selectors and management of the team little expectation of success in South Africa. J B G.Thomas wrote in a pre-tour article for the South African *Outspan* newspaper, 'We do not expect the junior Dragons to have anything like an invincible tour. I feel they will experience a hard tour and will do well to win half their matches'. Pre-tour, no one could argue against these comments, which certainly reflected our performances at home.

There was one last final trial for the selectors to make final decisions, a match that I and several other players were not required to play in. This enabled a greater number of possible tour members to be given a chance of impressing. The touring team of 28 was eventually announced and for me the elation of selection and the award of the captaincy was tremendous. I suspect that like myself, the other team members gave little thought to the pessimistic predictions of the press as to the likely tour results. For us it was the greatest adventure of our lives to date, to represent Wales and visit a county renowned for its awesome beauty and outstanding rugby.

The early summer of 1956 passed in a flash. We found the money to make our personal contributions to the cost of the tour and enough to give us a little spending money. We kept ourselves fit as individuals and had two weekend get-togethers at RAF St Athan and Bridgend Grammar School. There we were coached by Cliff Morgan, Russell Robins, Gareth Griffiths, Bleddyn Williams and Haydn Morris, all with British Lions' touring experience. These sessions were an invaluable opportunity to develop field skills, and to promote team bonding and team spirit, factors that eventually made a very strong contribution to the success of the tour. The last weeks before our departure proved particularly glorious for me personally. I kept fit by sprinting and my overall fitness could be measured by consistent times of 10.1 and 10.2 seconds for the 100 yards. These times were fast enough to give me the Monmouthshire men's title at Rodney Parade, Newport, and the Welsh Secondary Schools' title in a run on grass at St Helens, Swansea. Perhaps the race that gave me the most satisfaction, however, was to participate with the Olympic athlete and Wales' wing Ken Jones in a sprint relay team that beat the county record of 45.2 seconds. Ken had been my idol for many years at Newport Athletic Club, and had coached me at both rugby and sprinting.

They roared - and they sang. Malcolm Thomas conducts a choir practice.

Finally, the 19 July arrived and we were off. We had 14 wonderful days aboard the *Arundel Castle*, including a brief call at

Funchal, the capital of Madeira. We trained early every morning on scrubbed wooden decks, scrummaging, passing and sprinting. I enjoyed the sprinting as I usually came first!! God help any passenger who might emerge from a door as we sprinted the full length of the deck. This was also a period of team bonding as we all got to know each other well. I can honestly say that in those two weeks and during all our time in South Africa I never heard a cross-word spoken by any member of the team or management – a management that was always sympathetic to the needs of the players and captain. The other great innovation of the voyage was the formation of the team choir under our very capable choir master, Malcolm Thomas. It was to prove of enormous value to the team, which was to become almost as well known for its singing as its rugby. I should also mention at this point, the presence on board of four delightful young ladies of the South African junior tennis team returning home from Wimbledon, including the later singles' finalist, Sandra Reynolds. These lucky ladies had the full attention of 28 young men and if nothing else they taught us the words of two classic South African songs *Sarie Marais* and *Ai Zigga Zimba.* These were to prove an important addition to our repertoire in the weeks to come, especially as we frequently had to 'sing for our supper'.

The food onboard the liner was something that none of us had previously experienced, in both quality and quantity. Finally, it was necessary to self-impose diets or we would never have been able to run onto a rugby field, let alone play. We enjoyed the celebrations to King Neptune as we crossed the equator, dolphins playing across the bows of the ship, the flight of wandering albatross, and flying fish (one of which came straight through a porthole and onto the dining table at lunch one day).

Shore visits at Madeira (left) and Las Palmas allowed David Walkey time to meet the locals

Full of expectations, we arrived in Cape Town on 2 August, to the breathtaking views of Table Mountain but left that evening on the overnight train to Port Elizabeth, travelling along the Garden Route, past the ostrich farms around Oudtschoorn and whenever the train stopped there was passing practice on the platform. On arrival at Port Elizabeth we divided into pairs and met the family who were to host our stay. This was the practice throughout the tour, so that expensive hotel costs were avoided. For the team, it gave us a wonderful introduction to normal life in South Africa, especially as we stayed with both English and Afrikaans speaking families. From now on life became a whirl, frequent practice, visits to schools and a hectic social life. We had our first introduction to the traditional South African braaivleis at a citrus farm near Addo Elephant Park. Here we were invited to help ourselves to oranges and grapefruit and had our first close encounter with wild elephants. Here, also, the duties of captain really started, as I had to make my first major speech, a duty that became almost a daily routine for the rest of the tour.

Three days later we had another long train journey up through the Drakensberg Mountains to Bloemfontein in the Orange Free State. My striking memory of this journey was of the long train snaking its way up through the high passes billowing white smoke back across the open-backed carriages. Suddenly, as we slowly climbed up through fields of white arum lilies and red samphires, Dave Jones appeared jogging alongside our carriage window!

As far as success on the field was concerned, Bloemfontein was undoubtedly the turning point of the tour. Our first training session at an altitude of 3,000ft was murderous, but fortunately we had a couple of days to acclimatise. We came up against a massive pack, but our match performance was outstanding, despite losing our scrum-half, Clive Rowlands, 15 minutes into the second half. At last everything was falling into place, we were faster than the opposition and our passing and above all our backing-up was excellent. We drew the match, but had led with five minutes to go despite playing the latter part of the second half with only 13 men. Finally, the referee gave a very dubious penalty decision, for a scrummage infringement, directly in front of our posts and blew the final whistle immediately the kick went over. The tide had certainly turned and we went on to record six straight victories.

The fifth game of the tour at Potchefstroom was particularly memorable for me because for this match and the remaining three fixtures I switched from playing prop forward to number 8. Promotion or demotion? I was never told, but I enjoyed the four matches I played there, as it gave me more energy to run in open play.

Towards the end of the tour our management had been approached by the South African Schools Union to play one extra match in Cape Town – an international against South Africa. The management consulted me and other team members in their usual considerate and democratic manner, but it was an unanimous decision that such a match was impossible. This decision was taken, not because we were afraid of defeat, but because we were simply too tired. This match if it were ever to have taken place, should have been arranged for about the time of the Ellis Park match when we were at our peak.

Typical of our popularity was the time we left Kimberley on the long overnight train journey to Cape Town with an evening change of trains at Johannesburg. To our amazement we were met on the platform at Johannesburg in the late evening, by dozens of friends and well wishers. The platform became the scene of an impromptu recital of Welsh and South

African airs and by the time the Cape Town train slowly pulled out to the strains of 'We'll keep a welcome in the hillsides' from Young Dragons, hanging out of the carriage windows, there was not a dry eye on the platform or on the train – a remarkable farewell.

Our last lap took us back to Cape Town, travelling by car the short distance from the picturesque town of Wellington, set amongst vineyards and beautiful mountain scenery. We were really grateful that the previous day's match against Boland had been our last as I don't think we could have kept going on adrenalin much longer. We finished the tour as we had begun with another day of school visits, a final farewell braaivleis in Cape Town and on 31 August we departed for fourteen days of relaxation aboard the *Carnarvon Castle*. There was a short stop at Las Palmas on Grand Canaria en route before we docked at Southampton on 14 September. We had travelled over 4,000 miles, spent over 100 hours in trains, over 15 hours in buses and cars, all in the space of 25 days. I ask myself today what modern rugby team would be expected to work to such an itinerary.

Now fifty years later it is in some ways easier to reflect why the Young Dragons were so successful. In a nutshell, the answer was team spirit. To start with, I would like to pay tribute to the management team who were superb before and during the tour. They were sympathetic, considerate and always put the needs of the team first. This in itself led to a happy tour. Their team selections were sensible, and they always tried to give all touring players an opportunity to play whilst at the same time trying to produce a well balanced team with a chance of winning. Our two principal coaches were G J 'Guto' Davies and Gwynfor Davies who worked tirelessly on the practice field with ample backup from Percy Williams and Rowley Jones while Ned Gribble and H.S Warrington both made their contributions. I must pay tribute to our South African tour manager Mr.Claude Mullan, a headteacher from Springs High School in the Eastern Transvaal. He was a quiet, unassuming man who was always available to advise or offer help to any member of the team.

Finally, to the players themselves. As a team they were a pleasure to captain, both on and off the field. There was never a word of dissent to myself or the management and every one of them was always prepared to respond with extra effort when asked to do so. This was not a team filled with highly gifted individuals, as our pre- tour results showed. We did not have a Cliff Morgan, JPR Williams or Barry John, but we did have 28 willing young men, who gave everything they had to the team effort. As their match fitness improved, so did their ability and speed about the field. We were quick to the breakdown and the level of backing up I have rarely seen since, in any team. In some respects the Young Dragons of 1956 played a type of rugby that we saw more recently from the Welsh team of 2005. It was fast and open and we were capable of outplaying physically stronger and bigger teams by speed and backing up. You never had to worry if you passed the ball backwards – there would not be someone behind you to take it.

Yes, for all of us who went, the tour of 1956 was a time to remember with pride. For me personally, and I suspect for many other members of the team, it represents a period of our lives that was profound in shaping our characters for the future, and, fifty years on, its memories are as fresh as if it took place yesterday.

PART 1 THE BACKGROUND

All That Is Best In Manly Sport . . .

In the summer of 1956, a team of 28 players and six officials sailed out of Southampton on a great adventure that was to cement their place as true pioneers in the annals of Welsh rugby. The Young Dragons, as they came to be known, were venturing into territory that no other team from the Principality – national, club or composite – had ever been before. They were about to undertake an historic eight-match tour of South Africa. There was no shortage of sceptics in and around the corridors of power of the game in Wales who said they should not be going. Their pessimism was laced with gloomy forebodings of a succession of heavy defeats that would do nothing positive for the image of our national game at home or abroad. Others had even questioned the financial logistics of such an expensive expedition. Yet long before they left home the enterprising and visionary teachers behind the Young Dragons had dispelled those doubts, not only raising the necessary resources but also with money to spare after an intensive fund-raising campaign that was a model of its type – and one that others might learn from. There were many more lessons provided by the exploits of these young players. Two months later they would return from a triumphant tour that, despite all the obstacles, brought not embarrassment but fresh glory to the sport and, indeed, the schools in Wales.

The Young Dragons were the torch-bearers for the Welsh Secondary Schools, the national team of 18- and 19-year-olds that for seasons past had captured the imagination of the hungry post-war rugby audiences. Since 1945 alone some of the greatest names of Welsh rugby had cut their representative teeth in the annual matches against Yorkshire, the full England side and France before achieving fame in the senior game. Lewis Jones, Bryn Meredith, Gareth Griffiths, Keith Rowlands and R C C Thomas were just a handful of the dozens who graduated from secondary schools to senior Wales' teams over the course of a decade. By 1956, and despite one or two disappointing results, secondary schools' rugby in Wales was at its zenith; the epitome of aspiring excellence and honest endeavour that drew many admirers. For the latter, if not the nervous administrators, the tour to South Africa by the Young Dragons was the natural extension of everything that had been achieved to date.

The Welsh Secondary Schools had first played representative and international matches in 1924. On its establishment the previous year the constitution of the WSSRU had clearly outlined its *raison d'etre*: 'to link up the Public and Secondary Schools in Wales and to encourage in them sociability, comradeship, honour, a deep and lasting interest in Rugby Football, and all that is best in manly sport.' Obviously, this would include the organisation of inter-school matches (sixteen schools were affiliated almost immediately), but beyond that there was the laudable intention to organise international matches. The lycées of France readily agreed to an annual fixture and, with the reluctance of the Rugby Football Union to commit itself to the principle of a national team at that stage, an invitation was extended to Yorkshire, then the hotbed of English rugby. So began a happy series of matches that eventually found their own niche on the sporting calendar: the Yorkshire match every New Year and France at Easter so that both fixtures coincided with the school holidays. The perceived professionalising of the game in France meant that, as with senior rugby, the cross-channel fixture was lost in the 1930s but order was restored in 1945 with the added bonus of an annual game against England as well as Yorkshire. By then, too, nearly one hundred schools were affiliated to the national organisation.

By the 1950s the 'Secondary Schools' match' had a unique place in the hearts and minds of the younger generation of rugby fans as well as their families. The home matches were invariably staged on Saturday afternoons at Cardiff Arms Park with attendances often approaching 25,000. A large proportion of the crowd was made up of official school parties that had descended in organised coach loads on the capital city. Their excursions were rarely disappointing. Secondary Schools' rugby was synonymous with flair and sweeping back play and it was never difficult to spot the budding stars of the game. In successive seasons Glyn Davies, Carwyn James, Cliff Morgan and Ken Richards, all of them future senior internationals, occupied the fly-half position; likewise, the captains included Russell Robins, Onllwyn Brace and Meirion Roberts. The results usually matched the performances, with England beaten six times in a row and France, the real yardstick of achievement, succumbing to a hat-trick of defeats between 1951 and 1953.

Ironically, as the first ideas of a possible overseas tour were being discussed in 1955, both England and France beat Wales that spring. But by then the impetus for such a ground-breaking trip was already gaining a momentum of its own.

The first steps had been made by a Welsh exile living in South Africa – Levi Jones, a native of Pontardawe, head teacher of a school in the Transvaal and all-round rugby fanatic. Early in 1953 Jones had written to the executive committee of the WSSRU suggesting a tour by South African schoolboys to Wales – and with the possibility of a reciprocal visit. His approach fell on stony ground. As one member of the executive noted, 'It seemed a wild dream of a man with nothing much to do to while away the long hours of his retirement.' But Levi Jones was persistent. Money (and obviously time!) seemed no object to him as he travelled twice to Wales to convince the committee of the merits and feasibility of the project. His 'final aim in life', as he put it, was to establish contact between the rugby-playing schoolboys of the two countries he loved. Eventually, his overtures bore fruit. In January 1954 the executive committee finally accepted his suggestion that the schools of Wales would act as hosts to a party of 30 boys and four officials from the Eastern Transvaal. A programme of matches, culminating with a game against Wales in Newport, would be drawn up for the late winter of 1955. A return trip to South Africa was still a pipe dream…but the seeds of a great adventure had unknowingly been sown.

The South African Schools' Tour of 1955

Despite all the original reservations, once the incoming tour by the South African High Schools was agreed in principle, the arrangements were planned in great detail and completed in an impressively business-like manner. If Levi Jones had a counterpart in Wales, it was T Rowley Jones of Brynmawr. A much younger man than his namesake – he was still only 39 in January 1955 – Rowley already had an admirable track record in his services to schools' rugby in Wales. He had been a committee member for several years and was also a past chairman. Now, he was undoubtedly the driving force for the tour within the executive committee. We shall see later how his vision and refusal to take no for an answer benefited all who came into contact with him, with no better example than the reality of the Young Dragons' tour. But in 1954 Rowley devoted a considerable amount of time and energy to dotting every 'i' and crossing every 't' as the itinerary for the visitors took shape. He was an obvious choice to take on the responsibility of tour secretary and he was supported by a sub-committee of other dedicated teachers. They were Percy Williams (Abertillery), Dan Jones (Merthyr), Walter Lock (Cardiff), W R Davies (Maesteg), Gwynfor Davies (Carmarthen) and Idris Cleaver (Pembroke Dock).

The first priority, of course, was to finalise the itinerary. It was soon agreed that the party would start their visit in the west and gradually travel across South Wales until they played their final game at Newport. Along the way there would be designated 'host' towns at Tenby, Carmarthen, Port Talbot, Merthyr, Abertillery, Cardiff and, finally, Newport – and with an approximate stop-over of three to four days at each place. A factor in the choice of venues was that there should be a balance between agricultural, industrial and seaside communities so that the visitors could experience the full range of Welsh culture. It was the sole responsibility of each sub-committee member to organise entertainment and billeting in his particular area. Though they may not have fully appreciated the implications at the time, what was being devised was a prototype that, on a much greater scale in terms of distance, would be adopted by the South African hosts in 1956.

The South African High Schools team, with Rowley Jones (centre in blazer) at another stopover in Wales in 1955.

Whatever enthusiasm was generated by the sub-committee members, it does appear that there were still some dissenting voices on the wider executive body. In his own journal that faithfully records the tours of 1955 and 1956, Gwynfor Davies noted: 'The big worry about this tour [of 1955] was one of finance. The parent body of the WSSRU granted £350 towards the expenses which were envisaged, and still there were cries from certain executive members that this new, and therefore untried, project was certain to end up as a big drain on the Union's resources.' Davies and his colleagues, under the efficient guidance of Rowley Jones, were determined that such a scenario would not materialise. By the New Year of 1955 all areas had their various programmes worked out and those involved were convinced that the tour would be a success. One thing that they couldn't legislate for was the weather and, as luck would have it, January came in with a big freeze which rendered playing conditions impossible. But by the time the South Africans arrived in Cardiff on 21 January the weather had relented. Indeed, a mild (but wet) spell was about to envelop South Wales for the duration of the tour. The gods were smiling on the project after all.

Rowley Jones accurately set the tone of the tour in his goodwill message to the visitors. He wrote:

> 'This tour of Wales by your High Schools…is unique not only to our Union but, we think, to any schools' organisation. We are proud to be pioneers of such a project and extend to you our most sincere welcome. Our country has a great rugger tradition and it is felt that the WSSRU has contributed in some small way to it. We are mindful, however, of the high esteem with which all South Africans are held. We know the great skill with which the game is played by your countrymen. The success and skill of your senior teams must only have been achieved by careful and scientific coaching in the schools. Our teams will be faced with a formidable task when they take the field against you….Apart from rugby football our little land has some small reputation for the warmth of its hospitality. I am sure you will experience this to the full in the Welsh homes in which you will stay. We are going to show you as much as we can in the short time at our disposal…We want you to carry back to South Africa as many pleasant memories of Wales as possible. On behalf of all the people of Wales I extend to you a warm and sincere welcome on this first visit to our country. We hope you will benefit physically, socially and educationally and that the many friends you make will inspire you to visit us again in the not too distant future.'

These were perfect sentiments and uncannily presaged what was to follow both on and off the field. The final itinerary cleverly balanced formal and informal occasions. The first four days in Pembrokeshire were typical of the rest of the tour: a civic welcome by the Lord Mayor of Tenby; a team run-out at the local grammar school; a visit to St David's Cathedral; a tour of Manorbier Castle; lunch with a rotary club; and on Tuesday 25 January at 2.30pm the opening match against Pembrokeshire Schools kicked-off. Seven more matches would follow by 12 February and, if there was a disappointment, it was that the playing standards were slightly below par. Yet it must be remembered that the tour party had been selected from only three schools in the Eastern Transvaal – Springs Boys High, Huguenot Hoerskool and Heidelberg Herschel – and their limitations, essentially in their back play, prevented

Maurice Palmer (left) meets up with South African captain Rob Lombard at a reunion in Buckinghamshire in 2004. Their respective better halves are Bubbles Lombard (front left) and Jessie Palmer.

them from capitalising on the expected power in their pack. Yet they were well led by an impressive full back, Rob Lombard, and an excellent manager in the referee, T H 'Bert' Woolley.

The opening game against Pembrokeshire at Heywood Lane, Tenby, was full of incident. The tourists' right wing, Andre Basson, sprinted over for the first converted try after only five minutes. One of his team-mates watching from the grandstand was overheard saying, 'That's the first of many' and as the game continued with the home side reportedly 'swept off their feet and literally pulverised by the opposition' there seemed no reason to doubt the boast. However, the Pembrokeshire team was far from finished, with the *Cymric Times* further reporting, 'They seemed to realise that their visitors from overseas were not the supermen they were made out to be, but simply honest to goodness footballers'. And so as the game wore on a measure of equality crept in and set up the most dramatic of endings. Two Young Dragons of the future, Maurice Palmer and John Ebsworth, took centre-stage as Pembrokeshire levelled the scores on the brink of injury time. It was Palmer's punt from a loose maul that eluded the visitors' defence and Ebsworth who pounced on it for the vital touchdown. A conversion that just scraped over the cross bar ensured a satisfactory 5-all draw.

The pattern of the game at Tenby proved to be a forerunner of what was to follow during the rest of the tour. The South Africans lost 3-nil against West Wales at Carmarthen Park and every game after that was close fought. By the time they reached Newport for the tour climax against Wales their record in six matches was two wins, one defeat and three draws. But wherever they went they attracted respectable crowds of four to six thousand and at Newport the attendance was a very impressive 15,000. That afternoon there were four players in the Wales' team who would eventually tour South Africa in 1956 – Rhys Thomas and Alan Rees in the centre, Dewi Robinson at fly half, and Allan Williams in the back row.

The West Wales and South African High Schools teams at Carmarthen Park before the kick-off on 27 January 1955.

Also included was the future Wales captain and star of two Lions' tours, Alun Pask. Wales won the game 6-3 thanks to tries from both wings, Bryan Woolley and John Jeffreys. More importantly, in financial as well as educational terms, the tour had been an overwhelming success. Far from losing money, it had realised a profit of £1,368 14s 6d. Suddenly, the proposal for a reciprocal visit to South Africa the following year seemed more achievable than ever.

Making It Work

With the South African schoolboys heading for home, attention now switched back to the committee rooms as the champions of the projected return trip faced up to the not inconsiderable lobbying and politicking that would be required to once again convince the doubters. A formal resolution approving a tour in 1956 would need to be voted on by the full executive committee. Once again it was T Rowley Jones who refused to allow the matter to be pushed aside and forgotten. With a third of the money already in the bank he pleaded for the chance to raise the extra finances required. Unbelievably, some committee members even at that stage had other plans for the profits from the 1955 tour. Rowley Jones later wrote, 'I was devastated when my application for the £1,300 to be made available for a reciprocal tour was initially turned down by the executive committee. There were those – the majority in fact – who felt that this sum of money belonged to all the affiliated schools and should not be used solely for the use of those who might be involved in the tour of South Africa. Financially, then, we started from scratch apart from a small sum that was granted for postages.'

To their credit, the doubters on the executive eventually overcame their misgivings and gave Rowley Jones the green light to push ahead with the project, though the suspicion remains that in some cases they did so believing the financial shortfall would never be overcome and the tour would never take place. If so, they were wrong on both counts. What was about to get underway in the early spring of 1955 was one of the most remarkable and inspired episodes of fund-raising in the annals of the sport. Rowley Jones and his wife Mary masterminded the whole operation from the family home in King Edward Road, Brynmawr. Over the course of the next 18 months they worked through the telephone directory trying to identify potential sponsors, addressed and posted 8,000 appeal letters, acknowledged and issued receipts for 700 donations, and – their big idea that certainly paid off – sent raffle tickets to every school in Wales and offering autographed rugby balls as prizes. When the ticket stubs were returned, many of them were separated and put into the drum by the school prefects of Brynmawr in readiness for the eventual draw, a piece of enterprise probably illegal and definitely deemed politically incorrect these days but at that time further evidence that an all-encompassing cottage industry was underway in Breconshire!

There was still a lot more to do. Rowley Jones realised that raising public awareness was a priority and sought the help of the respected and highly influential rugby correspondent of the *Western Mail*, J B G Thomas. They first explored the possibility of placing advertisements in the newspaper but quickly discarded that as being far too expensive. Their next idea proved to be the game-breaker: why not launch a public appeal, duly reported in the press, and then have the *Mail* publishing weekly receipts? The plan worked a treat. Soon, the first of 700 donations began to arrive. They revealed some interesting responses Realising that it had to be seen to be doing something, the Welsh Rugby Union donated £50; Cardiff City Football Club gave £100. We can draw our own conclusions from that. Meanwhile, collections were also organised at first-class rugby matches throughout the Principality. As the months went by, the target figure of £4,000 came into sight. It was also made more achievable by an agreement that local education authorities would make available grants of up to £25 for each player selected for the tour and that the teachers who travelled with them would each pay £100 towards their costs.

The final balance sheet read:

Appeal Fund (through the *Western Mail*)	£1,980 11s 1d
Schools & Draw for autographed rugby balls	£168 19s 10d
Collections at rugby matches	£166 0s 8d
Sundries	£7 10s 0d
1955 Tour profit	£1,368 14s 11d

All of this, together with the grants that would cover the £650 cost of the fare, meant that the tour was a reality at last.

The next stage was to give detailed thinking to the itinerary, the number of matches – and, indeed, players and teachers – and to the travelling arrangements. The original intention was to plan a tour of half-a-dozen fixtures and to take 24 players and three teachers. However, no fewer than ten provinces requested a fixture, creating a classic quart into a pint pot situation for the planners. There were only three Saturdays and four Wednesdays available, though at one point it was thought possible to squeeze in nine games. The final total settled at was a sensible eight games, thus mirroring the previous year's incoming tour from the South African High Schools. One fly in the ointment during the early stages of planning was the peculiar attitude of the authorities in Western Province. Rugby tradition suggested that one of the games should be played at the Newlands Ground in Cape Town, an historic venue in South African sport to rank alongside Ellis Park in Johannesburg where the Young Dragons would definitely be playing. It also made logistical sense as the tourists would first set foot in South Africa at Cape Town and then depart from there a month later. No one anticipated the reaction from Cape Town when Western Province were offered a game. It emerged that the policy of the local schools' union prohibited the selection of a schoolboy team on a provincial basis. There the matter might have rested but for an astonishing response from the Province's honorary secretary, Mr W Edwards, when the not entirely unexpected criticism of the lack of a Newlands' fixture emerged in the local press. In a letter to the *Cape Argus* he argued that the prospective tour was 'not a rugby one [but] an educational one with some rugby thrown in'. He added that a match against an individual school would have been acceptable, basing his stand on the fact that 'when the Springboks visit Britain they play individual clubs' – an interesting if not slightly illogical comparison. After further examining the minutiae of the draft itinerary Mr Edwards concludes with almost breathtaking pomposity: 'Might I suggest that it is unwise to label these lads with the epithet of fabulous monsters, or any other kind of animal for that matter. To us they are just a party of Welsh schoolboys coming out to see and learn something of South Africa at first hand, and to play an odd game of rugby here and there.' So even being named the Young Dragons was wrong!

He was suitably admonished towards the end of the tour by the doyen of South African critics, A C Parker, when he wrote, 'What an opportunity the Western Province Schools' Rugby Union missed of associating itself with a memorable tour.' By then it had emerged that an eleventh hour (and unrealistic) request had been made to the Young Dragons for an extra game at Newlands before they embarked for the long voyage home.

Thankfully, Mr Edwards was not typical of the South African administrators with whom their Welsh counterparts now negotiated. The contacts made during the previous season's tour of Wales, plus the continuing encouragement and guidance of Levi Jones, proved crucial. So, too, were the friendships nurtured in that Welsh winter of 1955. We can only imagine what embryonic master plans were being hatched in King Edward Road at that time when Bert Woolley stayed with Rowley and Mary Rowley Jones. Whatever they were, they paid off. With Western Province no longer part of the equation the eight games were finalised with impressive common sense. Personnel was settled at 28 players accompanied by six teachers chosen from within the executive committee. Once they had arrived in South Africa they would benefit from the assistance of Mr Claude Mullan, principal of Springs Boys' High School and friend of Levi Jones. He had been another leading figure in championing both the 1955 and 1956 tours and would now accompany the Young Dragons as they travelled across South Africa.

Long distance travel was always going to be unavoidable, and tentative enquiries were made to BAOC about flying from London to Johannesburg but the cost was prohibitive. So it was decided that a fortnight's sea voyage on the Union-Castle Line and disembarkation in Cape Town would immediately be followed by an overland transfer to Port Elizabeth for the opening fixture. Thereafter, all the players and occasionally the teachers would be billeted in private homes on the model used by the Welsh hosts in 1955. There would be no shortage of well-wishers and rugby fanatics in South Africa prepared to open their doors and provide a roof over the heads of these young players from another legendary land of rugby. Likewise, the touring party was keen to visit the schools to see their opponents in their own educational environment as well as attend functions that would include those organised by Welsh exiles. The ambassadorial element of the trip could not be underestimated. Somewhere along the line there would also need to be some time spent relaxing and sight-seeing and with this in mind visits were also arranged to the Kruger National Park and to the massive diamond mines at Kimberley.

As for the playing side of the trip, the two opening matches would be played at the test match arenas in Port Elizabeth and Bloemfontein and then the next two in the Eastern Transvaal, the province that had provided the touring team to Wales. After that it would be Potchefstroom followed by what always promised to be a major highlight, the game against Transvaal at Ellis Park in Johannesburg. In a demanding conclusion, the final two matches would be played within 48 hours of each other – at Kimberley and, as the party weaved its way back south towards Cape Town, against Boland at Wellington. In all, then, there were eight matches in 22 days and it was obvious that a playing squad of 28 players was by no means excessive.

The Final Preparations

With the policy decisions and administrative arrangements in place, the most pressing need, of course, was to identify the best players at 19-years-of age and under to represent Wales on what was truly a ground-breaking tour. The traditional trials' system of the autumn and early winter and international matches of the New Year of 1956 would be invaluable in underpinning every selection that needed to be made. For any player to be selected for, say, the Yorkshire match in January only to be dropped ahead of the summer tour would be a hard knock for such an individual to take. Thankfully, that was kept to the bare minimum with only one player suffering that unwanted fate. The selectors were clear in their own minds that, rather than stick with 15 to 18 players across the three internationals, they should be prepared to experiment more than usual to see as many tour candidates as possible in the most demanding match situations. This was bound to be a delicate policy to put into practice, with everyone mindful of the need to maintain standards, ensure good performances in keeping with the reputation and standing of the Welsh Secondary Schools, and, ideally, win the matches. Not every part of that formula went to plan.

Questions were immediately raised about one of the traditional bedrocks of the selection process – the constitutional decree that boys who have not taken part in early area trials cannot be considered for international honours later in the season. More specifically, this applied to the public schools at Monmouth, Llandovery and Christ College, Brecon whose players had not been available for several of the pre-Christmas trials. Rather uncharacteristically, the issue was sensationalised in the *Western Mail* in January when under the headline 'Tour policy may be a flash-point' John Billot wrote, 'Welsh Secondary Schools rugby officials must think they are sitting on a powder keg. Sparks could blow matters sky high when South African tour policy is decided on 18 February.' He went on to leave no one in doubt where his sympathies lay: 'On the face of it, it appears that the exclusion of the Welsh Public Schools would be unfair to boys who should receive consideration. It is not their fault that they did not appear in earlier trials. Schools officials are themselves to blame. Some boys have been deprived of honours by schools placing loyalty to themselves before duty to their country.' With the benefit of hindsight this is a curious state of affairs to understand. Technically, public schoolboys were as eligible as those in state education to play for Wales. Indeed, the pre-war teams had been listed as 'Welsh Secondary and Public Schools' and in the early 1940s there had also been matches between 'Anglo-Welsh Public Schools' and 'Secondary Schools of Wales'. It was equally true that it was the state grammar schools that had provided the vast majority of players for the national team – and almost exclusively since 1945. So perhaps the entire debate, as portrayed in the press, was a red herring.

When the team for the opening international against Yorkshire on 14 January 1956 at Newport was named it contained the usual quota of representatives from the grammar schools at Neath, Llanelli, Cardiff, Caerphilly, Bassaleg and several other long established hotbeds of the game. More significantly, three of the team – Rhys Thomas, Alan Rees and Allan Williams – had played in the international matches of the previous season and several others for their counties and regions against the South African High Schools. Rees was named as the captain. Over the years the Yorkshire team had often proved more difficult to beat than the full England and the county's most recent victory over Wales had been the 9-nil result at Otley in 1953. The following season's fixture at Swansea had been cancelled because of bad weather and in 1955, again at Otley, Wales triumphed 11-6. Now, as the long road to South Africa beckoned, Wales were about to lose again. The English county drew on several renowned rugby academies of its own such as Sedbergh School, Ampleforth College and Wakefield Grammar School and all had young players in a side that also included two future senior internationals, England's Roger Sangwin in the centre, and the Scot John Brash in the back row. At first the signs for Wales were encouraging. After repelling early attacks they took the lead with a Rhys Thomas try, converted by Ieuan Jones, but by half-time the visitors had equalised. In sticky conditions both sides attacked throughout the second half but Wales were shocked in the last minute when Yorkshire scored the winning try against the run of play. The 5-8 loss was a discouraging start to the international campaign but the damage seemed to have been addressed by the time that Wales next took the field against France at Cardiff Arms Park three months later.

Different age qualifications applied for the France match – all players had to be under 18 at the start of the season – and that, allied with a wish to see more tour candidates on the international stage, contributed to a selection showing eight changes from the team that had played against Yorkshire. A notable choice in the centre was David Johnston, who would become the first Welsh Secondary Schools' cap from the naval cadet base at HMS Conway in Anglesey. Another North Walian, Bryn Harrison, had played against Yorkshire, so all the indications were that the final party of Young Dragons would be truly representative of schools the length and breadth of Wales. The captaincy was passed to David Walkey. One of his fellow front rowers from Bassaleg Grammar School, David Williams, was the unlucky odd man out who would also be excluded from the tour party a few weeks later. Though Wales beat France 5-0, thanks to a 75th minute try by Johnson that was converted by one of the new caps, Dewi Jones, the first murmurings of criticism regarding the prospects for the tour emerged. One match report noted, 'A bone hard ground and strong sun gave the conditions they can expect in the Transvaal where most of the games will be played…but the disheartening conclusion is that on this form Wales will stand little chance.'

Privately, some of the officials soon to travel with the team were also worried. In his own journal Gwynfor Davies, executive member from Queen Elizabeth Grammar School in Carmarthen who would be a coach on the trip, wrote, 'Everyone hoped for a bumper year, with outstanding players galore, but it wasn't to be. Instead, the WSSRU was to experience one of its leanest years since the war. To make matters more difficult, Yorkshire, France and England produced outstanding teams. England, especially, were absolutely first class, with a powerful pack of forwards, an astute fly-half in [Bev] Risman, and a truly great right wing in J R C Young.'

Risman and Young would become fully-fledged British Isles test players against the All Blacks three years later. Wales had made a further six changes from the side that beat France but went down 5-6 at Gloucester, Risman's two penalty goals outscoring a try by David Walkey, converted by Ieuan Jones. More worryingly, England had played a considerable part of the game reduced to 14 and then 13 men. These were not good omens for what still lay ahead, but no one panicked.

The selectors had fulfilled one of their agreed intentions by selecting 24 of the 28 players who would go to South Africa in at least one of the three internationals. Of the other four players, fly-half Dewi Robinson (Mountain Ash GS) had played twice for Wales in 1955 and the front rowers Alwyn Morris (Neath Technical School) and Howell Morgan (Llanelli GS) had played for Wales under-15s previously and would later win their secondary schools' caps. The fourth was Clive Rowlands (Maesydderwen GS), who within the course of the next decade would leave an indelible mark on Welsh rugby history as captain of his country in all of his 14 senior internationals that included a Triple Crown and two Five Nations' championships. As the final preparations got underway, Gwynfor Davies summed up the situation succinctly: 'We were committed to the tour and we had to face up to all the criticisms and attempt to solve the many difficulties arising out of the season.' In the next three months between the England match and the assembling of the team at Southampton docks, everyone got down to business with impressive urgency.

The 28 players had in fact been finalised midway through the home international season so in one sense time was on their side. A closer look at the squad revealed that the Young Dragons were drawn from 17 different schools in the Principality with the largest representation shared between the grammar schools of Bassaleg, Caerphilly, Llanelli,

Mountain Ash and Neath who provided two players each. David Walkey was named as captain and proved to be a popular and successful choice. The youngest player, at 17 years 130 days by the time the team left Southampton on 19 July, was hooker Alwyn Morris; the oldest was Malcolm Pemberton (19 years 126 days).

The full playing squad was:

Full Backs: Dewi Jones (Caerphilly GS); Ieuan Jones (Llanelli GS)

Wings: John Ebsworth (Pembroke GS); Trevor Evans (Caerphilly GS); Clive Phillips (Neath GS)

Centres: Richie Griffiths ((Tonypandy GS); David Johnston (HMS Conway); Rhys Thomas (Neath GS)

Fly-halves: Alan Rees (Glanafon GS); Dewi Robinson (Mountain Ash GS)

Scrum-halves: Howard Merrick (Cathays HS, Cardiff)); Maurice Palmer (Haverfordwest GS); Clive Rowlands (Maesydderwen GS)

Utility Backs: Brian Skirrow (Cardiff HS); John Elgar Williams (Amman Valley GS)

Props: Neville Johnson (Bassaleg GS); Howell Morgan (Llanelli GS); Malcolm Thomas (Tonyrefail GS); David Walkey (Bassaleg GS)

Hookers : David Jones (Mountain Ash GS); Alwyn Morris (Neath Technical School)

Second Rows: John Davies (Cowbridge GS); Brynle Harrison (Grove Park GS, Wrexham); John Puddle (Brynmawr GS)

Wing Forwards: Leighton Davies (Garw GS); Allan Williams (Queen Elizabeth GS, Carmarthen)

Locks: Graham Davies (Ebbw Vale GS); Malcolm Pemberton (Newport HS)

The official team photograph of the Young Dragons taken at RAF St Athan.
Left to right - Front Row: D Robinson, Mr G J Davies, Mr P Williams, Mr H S Warrington, Mr E R Gribble, D G A Walkey (captain), Mr T Rowley Jones, Mr G Davies, A H M Rees
Middle Row: R D Thomas, D M Johnston, T E Evans, R Griffiths, D T Jones, I Jones, J E Williams, D L Davies, D C Phillips, H F Merrick, M S Palmer, W T A Williams
Back Row: D C T Rowlands, A Morris, B Harrison, W G Davies, B A Skirrow, M W Pemberton, J E Davies, D J Jones, D J Puddle, N J Johnson, M H H Thomas, H J Morgan
Absent: J L Ebsworth

There are some subtle differences in certain positional names between 1956 and today, especially among the forwards: 'number 8s' were locks; locks were, simply, second rows; and flankers were wing forwards. One of the features of the tour was that as it progressed through the demanding programme of eight matches, several specialist positions would be interchanged.

If identifying the 28 players had been a difficult task, in some respects it paled into insignificance alongside the rather more delicate matter of nominating the six teachers to travel with, guide, and oversee the players. The full executive committee comprised no fewer than 16 members – four representing Monmouthshire and Mid-Wales, four from East Glamorganshire, three from Mid Glamorganshire, three from West Wales, and one each from Pembrokeshire/Cardiganshire and North Wales. Committees don't come in half-measures in Wales but reducing the 16 to six was always likely to be, to say the least, interesting. Gwynfor Davies noted that, 'Now that everything was set for a two-month tour, we found that *all* members of the executive committee wanted to go, the original opponents of the idea included!' It was just as well, then, that there were six places to fill rather than three as first planned. A hard-headed conclusion fifty years on might be that six teachers for 28 players was what could be termed a generous pupil-teacher ratio but no one can quite recall how that number was decided on. Whatever the thinking behind it, nominating the first three of the six lucky men was a relative formality. The executive chairman was E R 'Ned' Gribble of Tonyrefail and its secretary H S 'Monty' Warrington of Merthyr and they were named automatically. The 'third man' simply had to be T Rowley Jones – a reward for his organising skills for the South African High Schools' tour of 1955 and his vision and will power that made the Young Dragons expedition a reality. He was also a long-serving officer in his own right and a past chairman, yet years later he confided to his son David that at one stage, presumably when only three teachers were envisaged, he had been tipped off that he was unlikely to be included. Thankfully, that never happened and he took his rightful place on the tour.

Eventually it was decided from within the executive that the other three places would be filled by Percy Williams (Abertillery), G J 'Guto' Davies (Bridgend) and Gwynfor Davies (Carmarthen). There was a sensible age spread across the six with Williams the senior man, having been on the committee since the 1930s and fast approaching retirement age; Gwynfor Davies was the youngest at 34. One oddity was that amongst themselves the six decided that no one would have specific responsibilities on the tour but that duties, as they arose, should be shared around. Confusingly, wherever they went in South Africa, Ned Gribble was described as the 'manager' and there was no disputing the fact that Rowley Jones was universally regarded as the 'tour secretary'. Other roles evolved from very early on, ranging from Monty Warrington being in charge of the players' pocket money (yes, 19-year-olds with 'pocket money') to Rowley Jones and Gwynfor Davies overseeing fitness training and coaching. At the end of the tour Ned Gribble, in his capacity as chairman, reported back to the executive: 'I would suggest in future that it might be better to arrange duties before the actual journey is started and to make each member of staff responsible for a specific part of the organisation such as baggage, first aid, training, etc.' In every sense, the pioneering Young Dragons were on a steep learning curve. Nevertheless, in 1956 the *ad hoc* management system worked well and contributed to the general happiness and smooth running of the tour.

One of the first tasks was to arrange two weekend training camps during the summer term before the team left Wales. The obvious venue was the RAF base at St Athan in the Vale of Glamorgan where necessary facilities such as a gymnasium, rugby pitch and accommodation were available. Two dates were set aside on the weekends of 1-2 June and 6-7 July. Subsequently, the second of the two proved to be unworkable so a one day 'get together' was arranged at Bridgend County School where Guto Davies taught. On 24 May Rowley Jones wrote to all the players, giving them directions to St Athan and clothing requirements, adding, 'It is imperative that you attend this weekend school [*sic*] so please give it priority over all other plans. If unable to take part through injury, attendance will still be necessary. Those who are able, will return home on Saturday evening.' This was only one of a series of letters mailed to the Young Dragons throughout the late spring and summer. The first, again from Rowley Jones, had been the letter conveying the most important information of all – selection for the tour. Bearing in mind, again, that several of the team were well past their nineteenth birthdays, it is amusing to note that these letters were sent to the *parents* of the 'boys' and that they were also required to sign consent forms for their sons to travel to South Africa. Among a host of regulations and instructions the same letter included: 'Money – You are required to contribute £25 towards the expenses involved. Your Education Authority are being advised of this and *should* they express a willingness to assist you with a personal grant I will inform you immediately. In the meantime I shall be glad to receive your cheque or money order for this amount. Limited money will be held by me and issued weekly – details later.'

Inevitably, there was also some advice on discipline: 'Six members of the WSSRU – all schoolmasters – will be in charge of the party. All instructions and regulations issued by them must be obeyed implicitly. Everything will be done to ensure the safety and well being of your son, but much of this responsibility will rest on him. Please instruct him accordingly.'

This was all good stuff and it actually got better as the weekend camps and the tour itself drew closer. Having put the parents in the picture, it was time for Rowley Jones to write directly to the Young Dragons themselves. In a three-page communication containing instructions about equipment ('Take one large case or trunk and one small soft case or bag'), clothing ('Every item of clothing <u>must</u> have a <u>name tab</u> on it') and, almost fatefully as it turned out for Allan Williams on embarkation day, passports (Information…from the local office of Ministry of Labour: OBTAIN THIS AT ONCE'). There was an impressive enthusiasm to emphasise important points ('LEAVE NOTHING TO THE LAST MINUTE') and reached boiling point when anticipating the social side of the tour: 'We shall very naturally be required to sing. Become word perfect in all Welsh hymns and songs associated with rugger in Wales. Anyone not knowing *Sospan Fach* and the Welsh National Anthem will be shot!!'

No one was complaining about these strictures, light-hearted or otherwise, and by the time the exhaustive letter concluded with 'You have just read these notes, now read them again and again until you are fully aware of all responsibilities and details' everyone must have been more than ready for the first weekend camp in early June. As luck would have it, one of the 28 players was missing. John Ebsworth was suffering a reaction from a smallpox vaccination and therefore missed the official team photograph. That was the only mishap on an otherwise resoundingly successful two days. The master stroke had been the decision by the tour management to invite several of the 1955 British Lions to come along and talk to the boys. The Welsh heroes who had taken South Africa by storm a year earlier, Cliff Morgan, Russell Robins, Gareth Griffiths and Haydn Morris, readily accepted the opportunity. The first three of them had been Welsh Secondary Schools' internationals only a few years before while Morris was teaching rugby to contemporaries of the Young Dragons at the nearby Barry Grammar School. It was always destined to be a success, but as Bryn Harrison from Wrexham says, 'Just being in the company of these legends was a big thing and a total inspiration for me.' Robins had particular words of advice that John Davies recalls: 'Russell told me to look at the ceiling as I lay in bed, imagine it as the pitch, and work out particular moves and field positions.' Griffiths was the elder brother of Richie, which was a mixed blessing when he arrived in South Africa and was always being compared to Gareth who, having been flown out as a replacement Lion in 1955, went on to star in the final three tests. The most charismatic Lion of all, undoubtedly, was Cliff Morgan and, to no one's great surprise, he enthralled the youngsters with his tales of life in the strange land, its rugby traditions, and the type of players it bred. In the months that followed and in the homes they visited, the Young Dragons, in turn, were expected to tell their hosts everything they knew about the magical Morgan.

The Young Dragons are a captive audience as Lions' legend Cliff Morgan outlines what they can expect in South Africa. The other 1955 Lions in the picture (and equally hanging on to Cliff's every word) are Haydn Morris (third left) and Russell Robins (far right).

Other more mundane matters also had to be dealt with as the weekend camp continued. Fitness tests were undertaken and future training regimes agreed; briefings on roles and responsibilities as rugby tourists outlined ('Remember you will be staying in a foreign land in the houses of other boys whose way of life may be different from ours – respect their habits and customs at all times'); and kit distributed. Each player was allocated a tour number from one to 28, both for administration purposes and playing jerseys. The system was fairly arbitrary, the first fifteen numbers given to the team that had played in the most recent international against England and the remaining thirteen based on positions from full back to back row. It worked well with one exception – D Jones and D Jones. David was number 9 (the hooker against England) and Dewi 16 (the full back after the first fifteen names). 'Dai was always getting my mail and I was always getting his!' says Dewi.

The second camp at Bridgend, having been reduced to a day, was less glamorous without the Lions. By now, the tour was less than three weeks away and, although there was some rugby played, time was set aside for the distribution of documentation, travel arrangements, team photographs that had been taken at St Athan (and charged to the players at 11 shillings each), and Welsh handkerchiefs (nine pence each from Abergavenny market!) that would be given to hosts and at receptions in South Africa.

Meanwhile Rowley Jones, along with the captain David Walkey, had finalised one other vital bit of equipment to take with them on the tour: the mascot. It was the executive committee that had agreed that the team should be known as the Young Dragons, but it was equally important that there should be something tangible to support the name. So four Welsh Dragon souvenirs were designed and made at the Wendy Boston Soft Toy Factory in Abergavenny and handed over to Messrs Rowley Jones and Walkey a week or so before the team departed. The idea was that, as with the old tradition of the senior South African sides presenting springbok heads to winning teams against them, so the Welsh Secondary Schools would have four such dragons available if and when they were defeated on tour. When they boarded the *Arundel Castle* at Southampton Docks shortly before lunch on Thursday 19 July 1956 they couldn't have imagined in their wildest dreams that only one such presentation was required. The Young Dragons were about to make history.

David Walkey receives the Young Dragons' mascot from Ken Williams, managing director of the Wendy Boston Soft Toy Factory, to the obvious approval of Mr & Mrs Rowley Jones.

PART 2 THE TOUR

Sailing South

The final Young Dragon to embark was Allan Williams of Carmarthen. A year earlier he realised that he needed a passport to travel across the Channel on a school trip to France; now, it had slipped his mind that one was required to travel 12,000 miles to South Africa and back by sea and land. The first SOS of the tour, sent from Cardiff as dawn broke, was answered by Mrs Williams in Kidwelly, and, with a little help from the local constabulary and sympathetic train timetables, young Williams had travelled alone, two hours from South Wales to the south coast, now clutching his passport and about to be reunited with his team mates and masters. Rowley Jones might have been forgiven for waving his legendary letter of instructions – 'leave nothing to chance' – at the red-faced forward. But he didn't, his private diary merely recording 'As we sat down to lunch the culprit arrived…'. The Young Dragons were a team in every sense as they settled into their temporary home for the next fortnight and anticipated the delights that lay ahead. First up, literally for some, was the Bay of Biscay.

The *Arundel Castle* set sail at 4.00pm and the English Channel was calm; the second day in the Bay was not so pleasant with at least a dozen of the players sea-sick. Thereafter, life on board became more hectic and much better. Daily physical fitness sessions were a must, overseen by Gwynfor Davies and Rowley Jones, and involving early morning running around the deck. As the ship sailed off the coast of Portugal on 21 July a structure was introduced over 45 minutes: 10 laps of the deck – approximately one-and-a-half miles; heavy drills for legs, shoulders and abdomen; and rugby training to include scrummaging.

What others among the 540 passengers made of all this can only be imagined. But the players (and allegedly the teachers) hit it off with at least some of their number! Also on board was the South African women's tennis team, returning home from the Wimbledon Championships and other tournaments in the United Kingdom. For all concerned it proved a happy coincidence.

As the voyage continued, various characters were making their mark, sometimes in the most unexpected way. Monty Warrington may have been one of the elder statesmen of the party, but he was determined to look the part while sailing the seas. Thus, one of his colleagues described him: 'Monty looks like a retired admiral – or a member of Merthyr Bowls Club on its annual outing to Barry. He's pacing the deck, gulping in lungfuls of "ozone" (as he says) dressed in a white cap and jacket, a white polo necked jersey, grey slacks and white plimsolls, Woolworth's pattern! It has been

Gwynfor Davies and Rowley Jones
set the pace on deck

whispered among the boys that the captain of the ship often slips down to Monty's cabin for advice, bringing with him any of his navigational problems....'

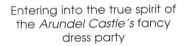

Entering into the true spirit of the *Arundel Castle's* fancy dress party

Allied to the daily training, there were other facilities, albeit modest to modern eyes, that alleviated the potential boredom of the 14 days at sea. The small swimming pool and sun decks were predictably popular; so too were the evening film shows, concerts, tombola, dinner dances and other entertainments on offer. There was a 'race meeting', the Arundel Derby, with the Young Dragons again entering fully into the spirit of things with 'horses' suitably named as 'Thick Head' or 'Red Herring'. The tradition of 'Crossing the Line' as the ship approached the Equator was particularly popular, with the fancy dress element and the ducking of 'victims' enthusiastically adopted. And, most of all, there was the food, readily available in quantities and varieties that was unheard of for these unseasoned travellers,

Crossing the Line on 27 July 1956 brought with it new experiences and ceremonies...

fresh out of homes that were only gradually recovering from post-war rationing. All the players testified to the temptations of eating too much – and all of them, of course, also reassured each other and their teachers that a rigid regime was adhered to and their weight and fitness never suffered. What was beyond doubt was that the training sessions did everything required to counterbalance excessive appetites. The general agreement in retrospect is that all the players were far fitter by the time they reached Cape Town.

The fourteen days at sea were broken by one stopover at the Atlantic island of Madeira. Their five hours in the capital city, Funchal, were gainfully employed, experiencing another new culture and, in some cases, avoiding the remonstrations of the locals. Impoverished young boys were happy to climb up the side of the ship and dive 60 feet from the top deck to recover shillings thrown into the sea. In Funchal itself the initial impression of a sub-tropical paradise as seen from the ship was at least partially shattered. Gwynfor Davies describes what he saw and thought: 'A great diversity in living standards was apparent: an old woman, her clothing filthy and in shreds, sleeping on the lawns that stretched along the promenade with its background of lavish hotels. Wherever we went we were stopped by men, and even young children, pressing us to visit one or another of the shops. Then we were accosted, literally dozens of times, by men of all ages with the age-old offer of "pretty woman, sir?" That set the seal of disillusionment for me, at least.'

The Young Dragons had survived their first experiences of an alien culture, perhaps a useful stepping stone before they arrived in South Africa. By early evening they were back on board and heading south towards the Cape. Now there was time to organise and practise another essential part of their tour: choral singing. The pre-tour appeal for a choir-master to volunteer had been readily met by the Tonyrefail prop, Malcolm Thomas. Though he now claims that he had no idea why he was the 'chosen one' he does admit that 'no one else stepped forward' and the baton fell, literally, to him and he rose to the occasion magnificently. The choir practised daily, eventually confident enough to give impromptu concerts for their fellow passengers. They also received the bonus of help from another traveller well-versed in musical training. Rowley Jones noted, 'We were fortunate in obtaining the help of a Miss Joy Wheldon to teach us typical South African songs. Apart from being a most charming young lady she was a very fine teacher of music and our choir not only acquired a new repertoire but also became a choir of a standard expected from Welshmen. We all felt deeply indebted

A fine body of young men taking the air on board ship

to Miss Wheldon and at the end of the voyage presented her with a small gift as a token of our appreciation.'

The first sight of Table Mountain as the ship approached Cape Town was generally agreed to be one of the highlights of the tour

In the early morning of Thursday 2 August, the *Arundel Castle*, having survived the Cape Rollers, approached the docks at Cape Town in the pre-dawn mist. Most of the Young Dragons were out of their cabins and admiring the lights of the port from 5.00am. Within two hours the necessary immigration and customs formalities were well underway. On the dockside liaison officers, radio broadcasters, newspapermen and Welsh exiles waited to greet and assess them. The real business of a rugby touring team now beckoned.

South Africa In All Its Glory

The first day in South Africa began in Cape Town but did not end there. Only eight hours had been allocated to seeing some of the sights and making a couple of courtesy visits to a local school and, ironically, the rugby stadium at Newlands. It still seemed absurd that after such a long voyage the Young Dragons could not stay in the city for a few days and play a game there. The initial intransigence of the local schools' union meant otherwise, though the indications were that by the time the touring team had arrived they were already regretting their policy. It was, however, far too late to change the itinerary. By late afternoon everyone would be boarding South African Railways for a 39-hour train journey to Port Elizabeth. Yet the team and their teachers were the personification of diplomatic ambassadors as they went about meeting and greeting local officials and dignitaries.

Their disembarkation from the *Arundel Castle* had been relatively swift and smooth, aided by the presence of the South African manager, Claude Mullan, and a veteran rugby tourist, Charlie du Plooy. The latter was a renowned 'baggage man' for many international teams over the years. He knew every trick in the complicated business of arriving in a foreign land and sidestepping all the bureaucracy involved. The players were suitably impressed as their new friend nonchalantly reassured customs officers and immigration officials that these young men and their teachers from Wales could

Claude Mullan (left), head teacher of Springs Boys' High School, and South African tour manager, with Rowley Jones.

be let into South Africa without too much checking and counterchecking. The afternoon edition of the *Cape Argus* reported what happened next:

'The Welsh schoolboy rugby team arrived in Cape Town today on a burst of song. Standing on the deck the boys practised their team songs, a performance that brought dock workers and wharf hands to a standstill....Mr Edwin Gribble said the team would play open rugby and would never close the game up. "In Wales rugby is an obsession", he said. "The boys are very fit and we have a good pack by schoolboy standards. We hope that we will meet up with many different types of rugby and we understand your sides are very strong." '

Predictably, the report went on to highlight the fact that Ned Gribble had coached Cliff Morgan from the age of 11 to 19 at Tonyrefail Grammar School, a point that would be aired and repeated endlessly over the course of the next month. The day continued with a tour of Newlands, a civic reception and a visit to Rondebosch Boys' High School for tea. Several Welsh exiles were understandably keen to be involved and did so by taking many of the party around the city to the three official venues in private cars. Other unplanned detours were also slipped in with impressive initiative. Typically, John Ebsworth, Allan Williams and Gwynfor Davies were chauffeured by a Mr Evans, originally from Carmarthenshire, and found themselves taking tea and cakes at his home, 'Plasbach', in the heart of the city.

At 4.00 pm everyone was reunited for the train journey that would take them nearly 700 miles along the Garden Route to the north east. The boredom of what lay ahead was broken by the scenery, ranging from the coastline at Mossel Bay and the climb to a height of 5,000

Another transfer, another railway station as the team prepare to set off on another long journey

feet between George and Oudtschoorn. For the first time the Young Dragons saw ostriches and other wild life and vegetation as everyone came to appreciate that they really were experiencing the trip of a lifetime. Eventually, Port Elizabeth was reached at 7.00am on the Friday morning. There was more singing on the platform, another official welcome and then everyone was despatched in twos to their billets in local homes, many of them transported in what they described as 'Chevrolet' cars, their mouths open at the unfamiliar standard of living they were encountering for the first time.

With only four days left before the opening game against Eastern Province it was wisely decided to waste no further time in getting on to a training pitch. So, in front of a large crowd at the Olympic Ground, the Young Dragons had their first run-out in South Africa. Once again, the local press were admiring: 'The Welsh schoolboy backs are fast and their forwards big and sturdy. Their chief weakness at the moment would seem to be their scrummaging. There was a tendency to pack too high this morning [but] for a crowd of boys who have just come out of an English cricket season and have had no rugby in the past three months, they moved with remarkable virility and with the hustle and bustle so typical of Welsh rugby.'

The backs go through their paces under a hot South African sun, with Alan Rees about to
receive a text-book dive pass.

Richie Griffiths, John Elgar Williams and Trevor Evans familiarise themselves with
a six-panelled South African ball.

The braaivleis quickly became a popular feature of South African life for the Young Dragons.

Debonair Dragons. Gwynfor Davies and
Rowley Jones obviously have found
something to admire.

Over the course of their four days in Port Elizabeth training sessions were interspersed with a full programme of visits and new experiences, including a citrus estate where they were allowed to pick and eat as many oranges as they wanted, a visit to a national park to see elephants, and, most memorably, their first braaivleis. Barbecues, by any other name, were not part of Welsh life in 1956 so we can only imagine what effect this new way of eating had on the visitors. Gwynfor Davies' diary contains an evocative description:

'This has to be experienced to be appreciated. We all sat around on the lawn in front of the house having drinks while a couple of the servants piled steaks on a grill over an open fire. When you felt like something to eat you walked up and took your choice – well or underdone! It wasn't a case of one steak, but as many as you wanted. These you ate with home made bread covered thickly with farm butter – delicious. Then a type of spiced sausage was cooked called a boerwars and this was eaten with potatoes in their jackets. There followed a short break for orange drinks and then, believe it or not, curried steaks were put on the grill…'

The sense of wonderment in this description tells us a lot about just what a tour of this type at that time did for the Young Dragons, rugby apart. As many of them have admitted, it truly was a life-changing experience.

The arrival of mail from home was eagerly anticipated and could even interrupt yet another sumptuous meal.

Match day at Port Elizabeth was like many others on the tour. The party was due to leave town almost immediately after the final whistle so that all luggage had to be packed during the morning. Then, while the players selected for the match relaxed, others went with the teachers to visit more schools. Some were more enlightening than others. One group went to Grey Junior and High School, a renowned centre of educational excellence and rugby nursery. While everyone agreed that the sporting facilities were exceptional – they included two gymnasia, half a dozen rugby and cricket fields, a 440 yards athletics track, several tennis courts and an Olympic-size swimming pool – they were also conscious that other schools in the city were less fortunate. To their credit, the group went on to see some coloured secondary and primary schools where, in one instance, a Dragons' teacher commented privately, 'The conditions were deplorable'.

After lunch the luggage was despatched to the station and there followed what seemed an interminable wait for the real highlight of the day. Rowley Jones noted, 'It was difficult to keep still before the game but at last we went to the ground.' The Crusader Ground where the match would kick-off at 4 o'clock was already filling up when the team arrived an hour beforehand. The eventual attendance was just under 20,000, the biggest crowd there since the Lions had played their fourth and final test on the ground the previous September. They had lost to both Eastern Province and the Springboks in Port Elizabeth, a bad omen. The Young Dragons fared no better, going down 11-19, though Rowley Jones fairly concluded, 'We did not deserve to win but the score flatters Eastern Province'. There was no time for detailed reflection on the disappointment because by 9.00pm the Young Dragons were back at the railway station, about to set out on another marathon rail journey of 22 hours to Bloemfontein. As they pulled out of Port Elizabeth, Gwynfor Davies wrote, 'There were many tears shed [and] what surprised us was that they came from the boys' hostesses: this spoke well of the impression that 28 Welsh schoolboys must have made in South African homes.'

The wild life was a major attraction for the tourists and here at Bloemfontein Zoo, several players plus Percy Williams and Guto Davies say hello to Kitzi the cheetah.

The arrangements at the next port of call, Bloemfontein, were very similar to those at Port Elizabeth. The 9.30pm arrival in the farming town meant that everyone went straight to bed, the players again billeted in private homes and the teachers, this time, at the Capitol Hotel. The first full day on Thursday 9 August included more school visits, then a trip to the zoo where they saw an extraordinary creature known as a 'liger'… a 600 lbs cross-breed of an African lion and a Bengal tiger. Once again, the Young Dragons were left rubbing their eyes at something bordering on disbelief. Other sights were more conventional, particularly training that afternoon at the Free State Stadium where the next match would be played and where the pitch was slightly softer than that of the previous week and benefiting from thick, brown and very coarse grass. Among the onlookers were a few of the opposition forwards, physically giants compared to the Welsh pack but whose limitations were to be surprisingly exposed the following day. As dusk settled and the day closed with a rather mundane visit to a cinema a Welsh teacher was overheard saying, 'Take us back to Port Elizabeth!'

The next day was more interesting, though what the teachers made of being taken out of town to see the National Women's Memorial we can only speculate at. What we do know is that the huge monument was erected in honour of the 26,370 women and children who died in British concentration camps during the Boer War. Nice. One of the teachers confided, 'The people of this state [Orange Free] still have strong anti-British feelings dating back to the turn of the century.'

Perhaps it was as well, then, that the match itself ended as a draw. The opening defeat had put everyone under pressure, with the selected team reportedly highly-strung in the dressing room before kick-off. They needn't have worried. In front of another large crowd, and despite the size of the opposition and losing Clive Rowlands with a fractured collar-bone, the Young Dragons led 9-6 until the dying moments of the game. Then a simple penalty goal awarded against them signalled the final whistle with honours even. Two hours later they were on another train, this time heading via Johannesburg for Springs where they were reunited with many old friends from the South African Schools' tour of Wales the previous year. With Bert Woolley, Robbie Lombard and several others waiting to greet them, it was almost like returning home.

One of the highlights of the tour now lay ahead. David Walkey speaks on behalf of all his team when he recalls, 'We enjoyed a wonderful two-day break in the Kruger National Park staying in thatched rondevals huts. Here our safaris sought out the Big Five, not exactly the same Big Five that we were accustomed to hearing about in Wales'. Perhaps not, but what they did see were zebras, wildebeest, baboons, giraffe, crocodiles, lions, elephants … the whole range of wildlife that everyone agreed contributed to making it one of the most exciting days anyone had experienced. It must have also been one of the most invigorating because on their return to the small market and mining town of Ermelo, the Young Dragons were about to begin an unstoppable six-match winning run that would justify (if justification was needed) everything that had been hoped for from the tour.

In Ermelo, the good life continued from the moment a police escort met the convoy of eight cars on the outskirts and, all sirens sounding, triumphantly guided them through the town centre to a mayoral lunch at the Merino Hotel. A hectic day proceeded with the billeting, a one-hour training session and a cocktail party, again hosted by the mayor. Treated like royalty, the team reciprocated the following afternoon with a marvellous performance against the Eastern Transvaal Country XV and a 33-3 victory. The crowd, long since having abandoned their hopes of a home win, roared their approval. And afterwards, for the first time, there was no rush for the railway station built in to the schedule. Instead, it was another of the popular braaivleis and, apparently, a 'merry party' that relaxed everyone involved. It was no cliché to say that the tour was well and truly 'on the road'.

Dewi Jones leads the team onto the bus as they head for the match at Springs

The next morning the team made the short return journey, again in a fleet of cars, to Springs where they spent the next six days, the longest stopover of the tour. This was entirely appropriate because it was from here in the Eastern Transvaal that the 1955 tour to Wales had been masterminded and now was the opportunity to not only meet old friends but for the Young Dragons to switch into full ambassadorial mode. Heidelberg High School, one of the three schools that had provided the players the previous year, was one of the first places visited. So, too, was the Cambrian Society where the welcome was predictably warm. Another victorious match against Eastern Transvaal was followed by a dinner and dance at the site of a gold mine and although everyone partied into the small hours they paid their dues on the Sunday morning at a church service that lasted 45 minutes – and conducted completely in Afrikaans with no concessions for the Welsh visitors. Rowley Jones admitted in his diary, 'Most of our lot just nodded off!' But there was now the luxury of no rushed packing of luggage, merely another two days in Springs from where there were day trips to the state capital of Pretoria to see the magnificent Voortrekker Monument, a tribute to the Boers of the early 19th century who had battled their way across hundreds of miles of wild, untamed country to establish a new homeland, and also the administrative buildings, the university and, naturally, Loftus Versfeld Stadium, the home of Northern Transvaal rugby where the Lions had won the third test in 1955. The Young Dragons would not be playing there but by now the prospect of another famous sporting arena was looming on the horizon. At the end of the week they would be running out at Ellis Park in Johannesburg, generally accepted to be the defining moment of the entire tour. First, though, there was the 120-mile transfer from Springs to Potchefstroom, another hard-fought victory against a powerful Western Transvaal side and then on to the big city with, it was reported by Gwynfor Davies, 'the lads in high spirits'.

The daytime temperatures were now regularly in the high eighties but the players were also more accustomed to playing at altitude. The results proved the point and the local press had certainly sat up to take notice. But could they go one step further and beat Transvaal? The preparations were again hectic. The day before the match was taken up with a visit to

Forest High School, where Levi Jones, architect of so much that had happened in the previous 18 months, was the former head teacher, a rotary lunch at the famous Wanderers Club, and then another mayoral reception. Saturday 25 August was earmarked to be another day of pack, play and depart. It was also destined to be a red letter day in the history of Welsh Secondary Schools' rugby. Team selection had been crucial. One noticeable change of emphasis had been an obvious decision to select the biggest forwards for this particular match. *The Star* newspaper beamed the headline, 'Dragons Field Heaviest Pack at Ellis Park' and observed, 'The Dragons have sacrificed speed in the loose for weight and ability in the tight' but also acknowledged that the side's two wing forwards, Allan Williams and particularly Leighton Davies (already described by one South African journalist as

Nev Johnson, Jack Davies and Brian Skirrow in front of the Voortrekker Monument in Pretoria .

'one of the best schoolboy forwards I have ever seen'), would be fast enough to disrupt any attacking ambitions by the Transvaal half-backs. So it proved. The final score of 21-3 in favour of the Young Dragons, including a 4-1 try count, was the most emphatic victory imaginable. Afterwards there were recriminations in the local press as questions were raised about whether the home XV had been truly representative of the best of Transvaal schools' rugby. Their post mortems had a hollow ring. Back home in Wales J B G Thomas in the *Western Mail* hailed a 'remarkable victory', adding 'No one in Wales even dreamed that the Welsh boys would win half of their matches. So far they have been beaten only once in six fixtures and have improved with every match.'

News of this response eventually reached the team in South Africa but by then they had already decided among themselves that they had achieved something special. The many Welsh exiles in the 20,000 crowd at Ellis Park had greeted their performance ecstatically and the celebrations had continued into the truncated post-match evening. Once again the team was leaving town soon after the final whistle, but not before witnessing memorable scenes at the railway station. Gwynfor Davies again takes up the story: 'At 6.45pm we all went to the station. It is impossible for me to describe the scenes on Platform 12 for the next hour. There were literally hundreds of people, Welsh and South African, milling around us – we just

The last game, against Boland in Wellington, had the perfect finale, with Malcolm Thomas and the choir in full voice.

Farewell to South Africa. The team on the *Carnarvon Castle* shortly before departure from Cape Town on 31 August

couldn't get to our compartments. It was just an uproar! [Eventually] amidst a tumult of farewells, desperate last minute handshakes and kisses as we pulled out for our overnight journey to Kimberley. We sat in our compartments – dazed.'

Part of the 300-mile journey retraced the earlier route via Potchefstroom and as the train stopped there, there were more astonishing scenes as friends made four days earlier returned to have one last look at the Young Dragons – even if the players were now stepping out onto the platform in their pyjamas. But the hectic schedule – and in some respects adulation – was beginning to take its toll on the players. David Walkey vividly recollects the beginning of the last week in South Africa: 'We travelled north westwards to the diamond belt at Kimberley to play Griqualand West. This included a fascinating visit to the Big Hole diamond diggings and a tour around the diamond extraction and washings mills. We were allowed to handle individual diamonds worth many thousands of pounds. The match itself – the penultimate of the tour- was played before a record crowd of 8,000 and we were comfortable victors by 14 points to six. A very satisfying result, but in the evening after the match, I for one, knew that fatigue was beginning to take its toll. I had played seven games in less than four weeks, plus the travelling by train or bus and all the other off the field activities. That evening I, along with several others had to drag myself to the after match reception and dance, and reluctantly, we left the reception for an early night, as soon as it was polite to do so.'

The great trek had become a test of endurance. One more 600-mile train journey awaited them, this time from Kimberley to Wellington and lasting another 24 hours. The small town of Wellington, 45 miles from Cape Town, was the perfect place to bring down the curtain on the playing exploits of the Young Dragons. They entered into the spirit of the occasion magnificently, with Malcolm Thomas, in full playing kit, conducting the team with the singing of *Mae Hen Wlad Fy Nhadau* on the touchline immediately before the kick-off. Then they went out to play open rugby in what was regarded as one of the most enjoyable matches of the tour. And afterwards the singing continued with a beautiful performance of *Sarie Marais* in Afrikaans, the song taught them by Joy Wheldon on the *Arundel Castle* all those weeks before. Translated into English, it includes the words,

> 'Oh bring me back to the old Transvaal
> That's where I long to be'

The Young Dragons of 1956 had undoubtedly left a big impression on South Africa, but now where they really longed to be was back home in Wales. The following day, Friday 31 August, they began their final journey as a team on board the *Carnarvon Castle*. Little did they realise that fourteen days later a series of very special receptions were waiting for them at Southampton, at Newport railway station, and all points west.

Even as they relaxed on the ship the eulogies were being prepared by the earlier prophets of doom. In the *South Wales Echo* Malcolm Lewis wrote, 'The Dragons set the Union alight by blazing their way across the Veldt with six victories, something which turned this team of "lambs" into a formidable, irresistible combination'. In the *Western Mail* John Billot was equally complimentary, praising the team for 'upholding the highest prestige and traditions of their country most magnificently'. Appropriately it was Billot's senior colleague, J B G Thomas, who had done so much to encourage the venture during the long months of fund-raising, who penned the most memorable tribute. Hailing the team as 'true rugby heroes', he concluded that the tour of the 1956 Young Dragons was 'an historic campaign in the game's history'.

The Matches

Match No 1: Eastern Province 19, Young Dragons 11

Played at the Crusader Ground, Port Elizabeth on Tuesday 7 August 1956

Eastern Province: P de Beer; G Jordaan, J Colley, M Bester, A Williams; G Rossouw, D Kritzinger; A Nel, R Mundell, C de Piesanie, F Minty, G Troskie (captain), N Bird, J van der Ryst, D van der Merwe

Scorers: Tries – Kritzinger, Jordaan, Williams; Cons – de Beer (2); Pen – Rossouw; Drop – Rossouw

Young Dragons: I Jones; J L Ebsworth, D M Johnston, R D Thomas, T E Evans; A H M Rees, H F Merrick; D G A Walkey (captain), D T Jones, N J Johnson, B Harrison, J E Davies, W T A Williams, M W Pemberton, D C T Rowlands

Scorers: Tries – Williams, Rowlands; Con – Williams; Pen – I Jones

Referee: S Featherstone

Attendance: 19,171

A marvellous scene as the Eastern Province and Young Dragons teams line-up in front of the expectant crowd at Port Elizabeth.

The opening fixture of any rugby tour is always a tricky proposition and this was no exception. The Young Dragons' difficulties began before the kick-off with the late withdrawal of Leighton Davies, one of the most experienced members of the full squad. He had been feeling unwell on the bus en route to the ground and was finally declared *hors de combat* in the changing room. Cometh the hour, cometh the man, and into his boots, literally, stepped a very surprised Clive Rowlands in the unfamiliar role of wing-forward. The rest of the selected team was an experienced combination, with David Walkey a proud captain and Alan Rees guiding operations behind the scrum. A second surprise prior to kick-off was the sheer size of the large crowd. Even the local schools' secretary, Tim Farrell,

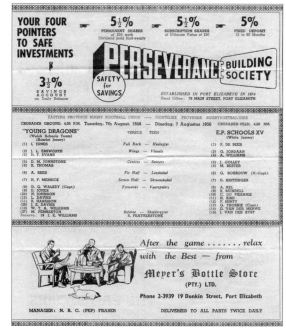

admitted, 'We expected 10,000, not nearly double that number.' He wasn't complaining. With gate receipts of over £800 the match produced a considerable profit. Equally important, hundreds of schoolchildren had a rare opportunity to see representative rugby and it was reported that 'cars with country registrations were packed all around the ground.'

The Young Dragons had proved a huge drawing card but in the early exchanges they found it tough to stay in touch with a determined home side. Fly-half Rossouw punished them twice, dropping a goal in the fifth minute and kicking a 35-yard penalty 15 minutes later after the back row was caught offside at a lineout. It was left to Ieuan Jones to record the first points of the tour shortly before half-time. A 5-yard scrum was called after several

Young Dragons' forwards had surged over the Province's line. When the home side infringed at that, Jones slotted the goal. But the side was reduced to 14 men when Jack Davies injured his right ankle; he bravely returned to the fray after the interval but was forced off again with 15 minutes left to play. Little did he know it at the time, but his tour, as a player at least, was over.

Allan Williams dives over for the first try of the tour.

In a great start to the second half, the tourists drew level at 6-all when Trevor Evans caught his opposite number in possession and Allan Williams pounced on the loose ball and raced 25 yards to the corner for the first try. Back came the Province and they seemed to have sealed the game at 16-6 with tries by Kritzinger and Jordaan, both converted by Piet de Beer. The Young Dragons were far from finished, leaving their mark on the match with a brilliant try, started in their own half by Howard Merrick and Trevor Evans and finished off, appropriately, by the rookie wing-forward Clive Rowlands and converted magnificently from the edge of touch by Williams. With Evans hurt in the build-up, the team finished with only 13 men and their opponents took advantage with winger Williams scoring an injury-time unconverted try.

Defeat was an obvious disappointment but Ned Gribble refused to be downhearted, telling the local reporters, 'The better team won, there was no question of that...but I am confident that we will give much improved performances when we are more acclimatised to the conditions.' The press, in turn, were less sure with one observer concluding, 'As they move northwards they will find young, virile and sturdy sons of the Veldt who will test their own forwards more and more.' The next game against the Orange Free State was already looming on the horizon as a test of character as well as skill.

Match No 2 : Orange Free State 9, Young Dragons 9

Played at Free State Stadium, Bloemfontein on Saturday 11 August 1956

Orange Free State: J Olwage; A Kelling, S Mandy, A Klopper, J F Lourens; P Carlstein, W Heunis; P Labuschagne, H Muller, W du Toit, G van der Wall (captain), H Terreblanche, J Moolman, D Jordaan, L Joubert
Scorers: Try - Heunis; Pens - Carlstein (2)
Young Dragons: D T Jones; J L Ebsworth, D M Johnston, J E Williams, T E Evans; A H M Rees, D C T Rowlands; D G A Walkey (captain), D J Jones, N J Johnson, B Harrison, W G Davies, W T A Williams, M W Pemberton, D L Davies
Scorers: Try - Walkey; Pen - W T A Williams; Drop - Rees
Referee: A K Volsteedt
Attendance: 12,000

Whatever questions were expected to be asked of the Young Dragons by the formidable Free State forwards were soon answered in style. Again their effort was handicapped by unfortunate injuries but to emerge with honours even on the scoreboard – and perhaps

In the shadow of the test match stadium at Bloemfontein, the six teachers and Claude Mullan line up with the Young Dragons XV that was about to perform heroically against Orange Free State.

even ahead in every other respect – was a minor triumph in itself. Beforehand, four changes in personnel had been made in the team. Leighton Davies had recovered from his illness and came back into the pack. Graham Davies, named for the tour as a back row lock, was selected in the second row. Behind the scrum John Elgar Williams played in the centre and Dewi Jones at full back. A positional change saw Clive Rowlands stay in the side but at scrum-half. Rowley Jones announced, 'We are still experimenting with some players and it will only be later in the tour that the one team is actually stronger than the other.' It was also an open secret that the thin air of the Veldt had caused difficulties in training but, equally, the pitch had been watered and that was a help to the tourists.

The Free State forwards were 12 pounds per man heavier than their opponents but to everyone's amazement were forced to give second best in the scrums. In the loose it was no contest as Leighton Davies and Allan Williams led the way. Within 15 minutes their team was six points up through a long range penalty goal from Williams and a beautiful dropped goal by Alan Rees. By half-time the Free State had pulled three points back through a penalty goal by Peter Carlstein. Much had been made in advance of the head-to-head duel between Carlstein and Rees, both fine cricketers and nimble fly-halves. On the day, the Welshman was supreme, one report lauding him as 'far superior'. In later years Rees played international rugby for Wales and Carlstein test cricket for South Africa.

In the 18th minute of the second half another player was injured and out of the tour when Rowlands fractured a collar bone. John Elgar Williams was also handicapped by an ankle injury. Five minutes later the scores were levelled when Heunis crossed for a try. As full-time approached David Walkey looked to have secured a famous victory for his team when he crossed for a great try but in the final scrum the Young Dragons were penalised and Carlstein

The Young Dragons' defence is at full stretch at Bloemfontein as Allan Williams, John Elgar Williams and Dewi Jones sweep across to cover a Free State attack.

made no mistake with the easy kick. Gwynfor Davies wrote, 'The crowd gave us a tremendous ovation and at the reception everyone acknowledged it was a moral victory for us.'

Match No 3 : Eastern Transvaal Country XV 3, Young Dragons 33

Played at Ermelo on Wednesday 15 August 1956

Country XV: E Groesbeek; J van der Merwe, D Byrne, J Jordaan, J Rossouw; M Wason, J Botha; D Krog, R de la Rey, G Steyn, A Smit, R Pelser (captain), N Britz, A Meets, J de la Harpe

Scorer: Pen - Krog

Young Dragons: D T Jones; D C Phillips, R Griffiths, D M Johnston, T E Evans; A H M Rees, M S Palmer; D G A Walkey (captain), D J Jones, N J Johnson, B Harrison, W G Davies, W T A Williams, M W Pemberton, D L Davies

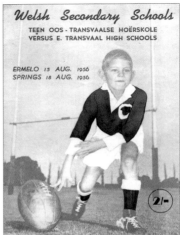

Scorers: Tries - Griffiths (3), Evans (2), Johnston, Rees, Williams; Cons - Williams (2), Rees; Pen - Williams

Attendance: 5,000

This was a game probably earmarked in advance as very winnable but a conservative team selection confirmed that the Young Dragons were taking no chances. A first win was now a priority so the same pack that had performed heroically in Bloemfontein was on duty. The three new faces were behind the scrum – Clive Phillips, Richie Griffiths and Maurice Palmer. Griffiths was to enjoy a field day. After ten minutes of forward attrition he opened the scoring with his first try from a cross-kick. Then he made the break that set up fellow centre David Johnston for the team's second try. Within another five minutes the tourists were 11 points ahead as Griffiths was again on the score-sheet. Alan Rees had converted the first try and with the game opening up it was time for him to display his intuitive fly-half skills. The local match report had an almost inevitable tone to it as it

Malcolm Pemberton takes on the Free State forwards.

proclaimed, 'Rees showed why he is regarded as the logical successor to Cliff Morgan when he jinked his way through to score under the posts.'

The home side's only response was a penalty goal by Krog, but tries either side of half-time (when the score was 19-3) by Trevor Evans left no one in doubt that the Young Dragons were running away with the game. In the latter stages they rammed home their advantage. Allan Williams, who had already converted Evans' second try, kicked a penalty goal from 45-yards

range before two final tries sealed the first victory. Richie Griffiths scored the first to complete his hat-trick and then Williams, himself, intercepted in his own half and galloped 60 yards for the final touchdown. The 30-points winning margin was a notable landmark; equally important, it was reported that 'in scoring eight tries the Young Dragons had enchanted the large crowd with delightful open rugby'.

Another successful goal-kick for Allan Williams, who went on to be the team's top scorer.

Match No 4 : Eastern Transvaal 0, Young Dragons 8

Played at PAM Brink Stadium, Springs on Saturday 18 August 1956

Eastern Transvaal: E Groesbeek; D Gravett, D Bornman, P Jonker, J Vos; E Steenkamp, C Lindeque; E Carshagen, J Nel, A Beukes, J Cronje, P Grey, P Uys, T Muller, O du Preez (captain)
Young Dragons: D T Jones; B A Skirrow, R Griffiths, R D Thomas, T E Evans; A H M Rees, M S Palmer; D G A Walkey (captain), A Morris, M H H Thomas, B Harrison, W G Davies, W T A Williams, M W Pemberton, D L Davies
Scorers: Tries - R D Thomas, D L Davies; Con - Williams
Referee: T H Woolley
Attendance: 10,000

Having tasted victory against the Country XV in Ermelo, it was important that the Young Dragons maintained their momentum against the full Eastern Province team in Springs. This was expected to be an altogether tougher assignment and so it proved. The management had commendably decided to be more adventurous in their team selection with Alwyn Morris and Malcolm Thomas making their debuts in the front row. Among the backs Brian Skirrow, on the wing, also made his first appearance and Rhys Thomas returned at centre. After the thrilling rugby three days earlier this game brought everyone back to earth with a bump. It was a clash of two very

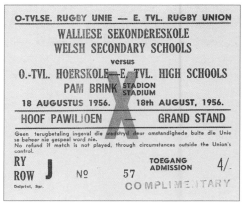

A match ticket for the game against Eastern Transvaal at Springs.

different styles – 'Easterns' intent on spoiling and keeping the ball among the forwards and the Young Dragons wanting to spin the ball wide but finding that harder and harder the longer the game went on. Yet they had made a promising start, continuing where they had left off in Ermelo with a try in the second minute. Alan Rees was again the catalyst, punting wide to the open-side corner where Rhys Thomas sprinted up for the touchdown. The try went unconverted and the score remained at 3-nil until well into the second half. Finally, Leighton Davies, who received rave reviews for his all-action display at wing-forward, linked up with his centres to score near the posts and Allan Williams converted. That completed the entertainment for the afternoon, though another Young Dragon, Brian Skirrow with an injured shoulder, was added to the squad's growing list of walking wounded.

Such a low scoring match had been unexpected after the heady goings-on at Ermelo and afterwards the reaction was uncomplimentary. One report referred to 'the long yawn', another to a game that 'dragged on'. The unlikely villain of the piece was the referee, Bert Woolley. Criticism of him, centring on his fussiness and apparent inability to play the advantage law (and his 'whistling serenade'), hurt the tourists as much as it must have him. Mr Woolley had been instrumental in making the South African Schools tour of Wales a

Lineout action at Springs. Among the Young Dragons in the picture are (left to right) Maurice Palmer (no. 22), Bryn Harrison (11), Malcolm Thomas (10) and Alwyn Morris (28).

marvellous success and had again been a genial host and guide in recent days. He was also a highly-regarded referee who went on to control major matches played by the Lions and All Blacks on tour in South Africa, but when the Young Dragons came to Springs it was simply a case of being one of those days when nothing seemed to go right for him.

Match No 5 : Western Transvaal 3, Young Dragons 8

Played at Olën Park, Potchefstroom on Wednesday 22 August 1956

Western Transvaal: E van der Westhuizen; R Laubscher, J Schutte, P van der Schyff, A Harrison; J Brink (captain), R Lombard; P Taaljaard, L Brink, J Swart, L Hattingh, P Otto, J Bothma, T Roscher, T Preller
Scorer: Pen - Brink
Young Dragons: D T Jones; J L Ebsworth, R Griffiths, D M Johnston, D C Phillips; D Robinson, H F Merrick; M H H Thomas, D J Jones, N J Johnson, B Harrison, W G Davies, W T A Williams, D G A Walkey (captain), D L Davies
Scorers: Tries - Johnston, Ebsworth; Con - Williams
Referee: P W van der Walt
Attendance: 9,000

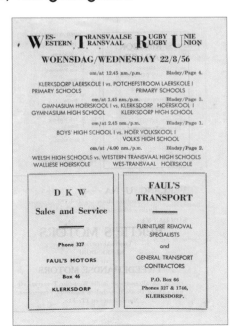

And so to Potchefstroom, where the rugby stadium at Olën Park had been the graveyard of many a distinguished touring team from overseas. A year earlier the Lions had started their legendary tour there – and lost. The Young Dragons were determined to improve on that and did so in a game that was far more exciting than the final score of 8-3 might suggest. For a start it featured one of the best individual tries of the tour by David Johnston. It came midway through the second half when the team was still trailing to a solitary penalty goal kicked by Brink in the first period. Receiving the ball near half-way, he jinked through the midfield defence, arced towards the corner flag, but as the cover defence came across changed direction again to score near the posts. It was classical Welsh centre play, albeit from a talented young man born in Scotland and mostly educated in Ireland. Now he really was 'Dai' Johnston! Mr Dependable, Allan Williams, converted, and later in the half a more orthodox back-line move resulted in a corner try for John Ebsworth.

The game was also memorable for the foot rushes by the Welsh pack, with David Walkey now playing in the middle of the back row and Dai Jones and Nev Johnson returning at hooker and prop respectively. The win was even more satisfactory when considering that a new half-back combination of Dewi Robinson (in his tour baptism) and Howard Merrick had functioned well and that Johnston was one of three further changes, with wings Ebsworth and Clive Phillips, among the threequarters. The only conclusion could be that whoever was selected for a particular match was proving up to the mark and serving the team well. However, with Transvaal at Ellis Park lying in wait, there were unlikely to be any selectorial bombshells in three days' time.

The now traditional pre-match photograph of both teams and officials at Potchefstroom.

David Johnston's spectacular try after a 50-yard break summed up all that was best in Welsh back play.

Match No 6 : Transvaal 3, Young Dragons 21

Played at Ellis Park, Johannesburg on Saturday 25 August 1956

Transvaal: B Steenkamp; J Els, L Phillips, C Dirksen, J Venter; M Ferreira, C Coetzee; A Koekemoer, L de Deugh, G Prinsloo, G van Niekerk, D de Jager, F van der Merwe (captain), B de Wet, P Prinsloo

Scorer: Try - van Niekerk

Young Dragons: D T Jones; J L Ebsworth, D M Johnston, R D Thomas, T E Evans; A H M Rees, M S Palmer; M H H Thomas, D J Jones, N J Johnson, B Harrison, W G Davies, W T A Williams, D G A Walkey (captain), D L Davies

Scorers: Tries - Harrison (2), R D Thomas, Palmer; Cons - Williams (3); Pen - Williams

Referee: D Birch

Attendance: 20,000

Without exception, all the surviving Young Dragons will now admit that the game they all wanted to play in was at the rugby citadel of Ellis Park in Johannesburg. In 1956 it had almost mystical status in Welsh rugby minds. Fresh in their memories were detailed match reports and flaky newsreel images of the first test between the Lions and the Springboks at the ground on 6 August 1955. The Lions, with half-a-dozen Welshmen in the side, had won 23-22; it had been watched by a crowd of over 90,000 and had already gone down in the history books as 'the greatest test'. Now the Young Dragons were following in the Lions' footsteps. They would be playing Transvaal High Schools rather than the mighty Springboks and there was unlikely to be a record-breaking crowd. But Ellis Park was Ellis Park and everyone wanted to be involved. Several, including Jack Davies, Clive Rowlands and John Elgar Williams, were ruled out by injury and minor knocks. One or two of the others might still have been considered too inexperienced for what promised to be the ultimate test of the tour. Certainly the selectors seemed in no mood for unnecessary upheaval and experimentation with what they concluded was their strongest combination. One thing the South African press got hopelessly wrong was their assessment that for this one game 'the Dragons [would] field their heaviest pack'. The forwards were, in fact, the same eight that had played against Western Transvaal earlier in the week. Equally, another press report that 'the Dragons have obviously [*sic*] sacrificed speed in the loose for weight and ability in the tight' was way off the mark. Behind the scrum, the midfield trio of Alan Rees, David Johnston and Rhys Thomas were generally regarded as the most experienced combination possible. What was interesting was how two of the youngest players in the squad, Dewi Jones at full back and Maurice Palmer at scrum-half, had risen to prominence during the course of the tour. Against stiff competition, John Ebsworth and Trevor Evans, won favour on the wings.

Ahead of the Transvaal game the training had to be spot on and nothing was overlooked, from lineout drills . . .

. . . to inch-perfect passing

The match was played in brilliant sunshine and in front of an estimated 20,000 crowd, the largest of the tour. The first score didn't come until the 13th minute, a penalty goal by Allan Williams, but the Young Dragons were already showing a willingness to attack from all areas of the pitch. They were temporarily reduced to 14 men after Alan Rees injured a leg when Rhys Thomas raced through for the first try, converted by Williams. To complete an excellent first half a second try arrived when Bryn Harrison charged down an attempted clearance kick for the touchdown and an 11-points lead.

Rees returned to the fray early in the second period and with the pack dominating up front there was a plentiful supply of ball to continue the attacks. Palmer stole away from a lineout for another converted try and now the lead was an almost unbelievable 16 points. Transvaal were saved from total embarrassment when van Niekerk charged over from a close-range lineout but the Young Dragons, appropriately, had the last word. Harrison was again in the thick of the action as he claimed his second try, unerringly converted from far out by Williams.

So history was made. A Welsh team had won at Ellis Park, and overwhelmingly so, playing a brand of fast, open rugby that their pedestrian opponents had no answer to. Predictably, there were some recriminations in the local press with assertions made that Transvaal had not chosen their strongest team. All that Ned Gribble and his colleagues could say was that fifteen young men from Wales had soundly beaten fifteen young South Africans judged capable, beforehand, of being good enough for the challenge in front of them. It was a moment to savour.

Match No 7 : Griqualand West 6, Young Dragons 14

Played at De Beers Stadium, Kimberley on Monday 27 August 1956

Griqualand West: D McLaughlin; J Slabbert, J Swart, C Nel, J Combrinck (captain); G Cloete, G Human; J Redlinghuys, C Kotze, J Minnaar, G Lodder, N Atkinson, C Philpott, A Dickson, P van Zyl

Scorers: Tries - Slabbert, Nel

Young Dragons: I Jones; B A Skirrow, D M Johnston, R D Thomas, D C Phillips; D Robinson, M S Palmer; M H H Thomas, D J Jones, H J Morgan, B Harrison, D J Puddle, M W Pemberton, D G A Walkey (captain), D L Davies

Scorers: Tries - Walkey, Phillips, Harrison; Con - Pemberton; Pen - I Jones

Referee: B Calitz

Attendance: 8,000

The two teams and officials before the match at Kimberley.

With two matches to play in the remaining four days in South Africa, there were still some loose ends for the management to tidy up. Most pressingly, two of the 28 players, John Puddle and Howell Morgan, had yet to play a game. That was immediately rectified with their inclusion in the team against Griqualand West. In all there were seven changes from the side on duty at Ellis Park. Ieuan Jones returned for his first outing since the tour opener at Port Elizabeth, Brian Skirrow and Clive Phillips were on the wings and Dewi Robinson at fly-half, and the versatile Malcolm Pemberton, outstanding in the middle of the back row in earlier games, now featured at wing-forward.

The crowd of 8,000 was the largest ever to watch a schools match in Kimberley and what they saw from the start was a spectacular display of running rugby by forwards and backs, lightning fast backing-up, and silky sharp handling skills from all 15 Dragons. In the first half the new look team threatened to overrun their opponents with brilliant tries scored by David Walkey, Clive Phillips and Bryn Harrison, the second converted by Pemberton. But they were achieved at a cost. Johnston left the field with a leg injury and Puddle and Skirrow were also struggling from other knocks. Playing against the wind in the second half, handicapped by the injuries, and, as Walkey reveals, feeling the accumulative wear and tear of so much rugby over the previous three weeks, the Young Dragons could only add a penalty goal by Ieuan Jones. Sensing their opponents tiring, the Griquas finished strongly with tries from Slabbert and Nel. Despite everyone's weariness it had been a spectacular game – and one more awaited them barely 48 hours later.

Match No 8: Boland 0, Young Dragons 8

Played at Boland Park, Wellington on Wednesday 29 August 1956

Boland: A van der Merwe; A Cruywagen, I Hugo, G van der
    Heever, J Stander; D Tromp, Le R Fourie (captain);
    R Malherbe, H Theunissen, J Kotze, G Greeff, P Meyer,
    F van der Merwe, A Louw, B Neethling
Young Dragons: D T Jones; J L Ebsworth, R Griffiths, R D
    Thomas, T E Evans; I Jones, M S Palmer; M H H Thomas,
    D J Jones, N J Johnson, B Harrison, W G Davies, W T A
    Williams, D G A Walkey (captain), D L Davies
Scorers: Try - Walkey; Con - Williams; Drop - I Jones
Referee: N du Bois
Attendance: 7,000

The final match began and ended with Malcolm Thomas conducting the choir on the touchline. Every Young Dragon knew the significance of the occasion and they wanted to leave, literally, on a high note. David Walkey led the team out for an eighth consecutive time in the space of 22 days, a remarkable record matched by Bryn Harrison in the second row.

The final team photograph of the tour at Wellington

All the fit players who had not played at Kimberley – Dewi Jones, John Ebsworth, Richie Griffiths, Trevor Evans, Nev Johnson, Graham Davies and Allan Williams – also took their final bow. A delighted Ieuan Jones was in his favourite position of fly-half. The happiest of tours was continuing right up to the end.

There was plenty of entertainment but no points in the first half. The Boland team entered into the spirit of a match full of movement but it was the tourists, according to R K Stent, who 'brought a gay, carefree spirit that helped to make the game the most refreshing seen in these parts this season.' Eventually the points came. Ieuan ('pronounced Yay-an', Stent told his readers) Jones dropped a goal and then sent a low, deftly placed cross kick for Walkey and Davies to chase. The skipper claimed the touchdown and Allan Williams' conversion marked the final points of the tour. In his tour journal Gwynfor Davies wrote, 'In the dressing room after this final game there was tremendous excitement – we had, so it appeared, won the hearts of the critical South African public and we were all now thinking of home.'

PART 3 *THESE WERE THE DRAGONS*

The Pride of Welsh Schoolboys

Ieuan Jones (Llanelli Grammar School)
Born: 28 June 1937 5'7" 10st 11lb Full Back/Fly Half   Tour Number: 1

Ieuan Jones was the ideal build for the archetypal Welsh fly-half, tiny and tricky, and he makes no secret of his preference for the pivot's role on the field of play. At Llanelli Grammar School he won Wales under-15 honours in that position, went on to captain the first XV and in January 1955 also led the West Wales team against the touring South African High Schools. But for the Welsh Secondary Schools a year later he played against both Yorkshire and England at full back. Not that he was complaining. Ieuan was a fine all round footballer and he continued in the role in his first two appearances for the Young Dragons before finally reverting to his preferred position when the curtain came down on the tour against Boland.

Ieuan admits that one of his personal highlights of the tour was scoring the first points, a penalty goal against Eastern Province in Port Elizabeth. It brought its own rewards: 'In recognition of that, a crate of oranges was delivered to my home address.' The South Africans were also quick to appreciate his qualities. The game at Wellington was watched by R K Stent, a senior journalist who had covered the Springboks' tour of Europe in 1951-52. He reported: 'In the game the outstanding man in the Welsh team was Ieuan (pronounced Yay-an) Jones, as stand-off half. Jones, a Llanelli lad, was spotted as fly-half in his early teens and was chosen to play for the Wales under-15s side. Later, I was told, he seemed to lose his confidence and was chosen [for the Young Dragons] as full back. Yesterday he reverted with great success to his old position…his darting runs and quick, swift passing recalled Cliff Morgan to many spectators – but I understand that Morgan is the model for all schoolboy fly-halves in Wales!'

Like his Llanelli Grammar School colleague Howell Morgan, Ieuan was also a good cricketer and athlete, captaining the athletics' team and being recognised as the town's

A packed Stradey Park in December 1963 and Ieuan Jones kicks a penalty goal for Llanelli against the All Blacks

Junior Sportsman of the Year. After the tour he entered Aberystwyth University to study economics and geography and then completed his National Service in the RAF, largely based in the records office at Innsworth. While there, he played both for the RAF and Cheltenham, then one of the foremost West Country clubs with a strong fixture list that included several games in Wales. When he eventually moved back to Wales to work as an accountant for the Wales Gas Board, Ieuan also turned out for Swansea, Llanelli Wanderers and, most significantly, Llanelli. In December 1963 he kicked a conversion and a penalty goal from full back for the Scarlets team that played the All Blacks at Stradey Park.

Eventually, Ieuan's career in accountancy took him to London where he was employed by the Gas Council, then by Mobil Oil and the Phillips Petroleum Company before his appointment as tax manager for the Europe-Africa Region. His later playing days had featured club rugby for Marlow and county games for Buckinghamshire. He also introduced mini-rugby at Marlow and became the club's treasurer and finance chairman. When he went on to coach the county's under-19 squad it could truly be said that the rugby days of the former Young Dragon had come full circle. In 1996 Ieuan retired, though he still continued to work in private practice for a further three years before returning to Carmarthenshire where he now lives near Llanelli.

Far from the madding crowd . . . a relaxed Ieuan enjoys his retirement

John Llewellyn Ebsworth (Pembroke Grammar School)

Born: 22 April 1938 5'10" 11st 3lb Wing Tour Number: 2

John Ebsworth's tour started badly: he missed the team photograph after suffering the ill-effects of a smallpox vaccination. Fortunately, this was not in South Africa but at the first weekend training camp at RAF St Athan and all of six weeks before the Young Dragons set sail from Southampton. By the time the *Arundel Castle* lifted anchor and sailed out of the docks in mid-July John was back to full health and fitness and looking forward to what lay ahead. He says, 'The thought of the sheer distances to be travelled plus the totally new and undreamt of experience of two weeks on a passenger liner was enough to make anyone excited. Nothing about it disappointed me though with all the food on board it was a struggle not to put on weight.'

He missed the team photograph but John Ebsworth made sure his passport picture was ready in time.

John deserved his moment in the sun, as it were, because he had proved himself worthy of selection after a series of impressive performances in the 18 months before the tour. As a sixteen-year-old he had played in the centre for Pembrokeshire Secondary Schools against the South African High Schools in January 1955. It was a notable debut into representative rugby as he scored the match-saving try in the last five minutes and was picked out in the local newspaper report as 'the best man behind the scrum on the field.' He went on to captain the county's under-19 side and in 1956 won the first two of his four international caps against Yorkshire and France.

The announcement of his selection as a Young Dragon was followed by the traditional presentations from the full gamut of local organisations – the Pembroke Borough Council, the Pembroke Dock and Borough Trades Council and the Pembrokeshire Education Committee – plus, for good measure, the local branch of Barclays Bank. So he was well-equipped in the material sense and he was also equally prepared as a player. He was a strong, big and quick wing and ideally suited to the hard grounds of South Africa. Not surprisingly, he was soon kept very busy, appearing in the first two matches at Port Elizabeth and Bloemfontein and five games by the end of the tour. The team's dedication to open rugby also suited his style of play and John quickly won praise in the match reports. Even in the tight match against Orange Free State it was noted that he 'showed great pace with limited chances.' His enterprise paid dividends at Potchefstroom when he scored the team's second try to seal the team's important 8-nil victory over Western Transvaal.

John with the team mascot

As with everyone else, the game against Transvaal left a big impression on John. 'Running out onto Ellis Park was the most thrilling moment of my career and the largest crowd I ever played in front of. The game was played at a tremendous pace and with great endeavour at 5,000 feet above sea level. The concern was that we would tire late in the game but that never happened. We had prepared well and the team played its best rugby of the tour and we won more easily than we had expected. Our technique, skilful running and greater mobility more than cancelled out Transvaal's strength and size.'

Off the field, John readily admits that visiting the vast new country was also hugely enjoyable. Before the tour he had been counselled by his father to 'steer away from religion and politics as topics of conversation' though he, in a rather deadpan way, adds 'not that they were on the top of my agenda.' Even so he betrays an impressive sensitivity to the unique problems of South African society at the time when he says, 'We were entertained by Zulu warriors dancing for us but it was also depressing when you thought about the fact that they were rarely able to leave the compound'. Other new experiences could be enjoyed at face value. 'We went to Kimberley and found ourselves handling £75,000 sterling in cut diamonds which was quite an unusual sensation and we were also told that near the old diamond mines it was rumoured that the locals still found the occasional diamond in their back gardens!'

Amusingly, there was also room for the odd *faux pas* with his fellow Pembrokeshire schoolboy Maurice Palmer never far from the action. He recalls, 'We were staying with a family in Bloemfontein and at our first evening meal we were asked to hold hands to say a prayer before eating. We could cope with that but then I was asked to say the prayer! Never having done such a thing before I had to dig deep and there was a long pause. I had a mental freeze but suddenly felt a sharp kick on my ankle from Maurice. That sent me into action. I asked that we should be thankful for what we were about to receive and now that I had bit between my teeth I went on to include all those who were less fortunate than ourselves. It was greeted in total silence. So much for my father's advice!'

After the tour, John had another year at school and won two more Secondary Schools' caps against Yorkshire and England. He never quite made it to National Service, failing his medical three times but the armed forces' loss was education's gain. He completed his teacher training at St Luke's College in Exeter where he played for the first XV and also for Pembroke Dock Harlequins, Llanelli (for two seasons) and Pembrokeshire. He taught for nine years and whilst at Northampton School for Boys he enjoyed more top-class rugby with

Back home - John, complete with an impressive collection of pin badges, arrives at Pembroke Deck to be met by his parents, civic dignitaries, the station master (with a very official cap) and, on the far left, another major figure in schools' rugby, Idris Cleaver.

Northampton, London Welsh and East Midlands. When his playing days were over he was backs coach at Northampton for two seasons (winning the highly competitive *Daily Telegraph* Welsh/English league title in one of them), was also coach and secretary to the youth team at the club, and a valued committeeman who later organised the first match sponsorship for Northampton and the East Midlands (for whom he was also team secretary) with Carlsberg.

His involvement in rugby and sport didn't stop there. He was a founder member (and, almost inevitably, an all-purpose officer) of the Northampton Dragons basketball team, ran in both the London and New York city marathons in 1982, raised funds for disabled charities through his participation in several half-marathons – and had the satisfaction of seeing two sons, Matthew and Jonathan, playing rugby for England Schools.

In 1972 John gave up teaching, though his wife Joan continued as a deputy head, and became an insurance broker and started his own business. In 2002 he retired due to ill-health and the family moved to the more agreeable climate in Spain. They now live in Alicante.

David Maxwell Johnston (HMS Conway)

Born: 14 November 1937 5'11" 11st 11lb Centre Tour Number: 3

The rugby pedigree of David Johnston has a familiar tinge about it to modern eyes: he was born in Scotland, lived most of his life before and after the tour in Ireland, and played for Wales. In 1956, however, such a background was a rarity but David's credentials as a Young Dragon were impeccable. He had, indeed, been born in Airdrie and began his secondary education at the High School, Dublin but in 1954 he had transferred to HMS Conway in Anglesey to study for his 'A' Levels. The teachers and officers at the famous merchant navy school soon realised that they had a gifted sportsman among their ranks. In Dublin he had played senior schools' rugby when well below the normal age and eventually captained the first XV in 1953-54. In the summer months he had won his colours at athletics and cricket and was the All-Ireland junior sprint champion for both the 100 and 220 yards. His prowess was quickly recognised at HMS Conway where he again graduated to captain of the first XV and the North Wales representative side. In the early summer of 1956 he was recording sub-10 seconds times for the 100 yards,

David Johnston in his cadet's uniform before he was mistaken for a railway porter.

setting a new mark of 23.4 seconds in the longer sprint and, for good measure, also winning the long jump and discus events at the annual sports. By then David had also won his international caps for the Welsh Secondary Schools, the first student from HMS Conway to achieve such recognition.

David's international debut had been against France at Cardiff Arms Park on 6 April 1956 and he marked the occasion by scoring the only try, converted by Dewi Jones, as Wales won

5-nil. One match report referred to 'Dai [*sic*] Johnston crashing through the French defence.' He was obviously by now a fully-fledged Welshman! A fortnight later he was again in the team that played England at Gloucester and from there his profile as a Young Dragon went from strength to strength.

In South Africa David played in six of the eight games, scoring tries at Ermelo and Potchefstroom. The second of these was particularly memorable as he broke through from the half-way line and was reported to have 'raced 50 yards for a spectacular try.' He understandably admitted later that the try was a personal highlight of the tour as was the experience of playing in front of a big crowd at Ellis Park, Johannesburg. The press photograph of him being carried off shoulder high after the final whistle at Bloemfontein remains one of the most evocative images of the tour.

A memorable image of the tour as David is chaired off after the game at Bloemfontein.

After the tour David went to London to study engineering. His rugby continued with London Scottish where he played for the first XV but injuries disrupted his initial season there. When he returned to Dublin he worked for J S Lister & Co., an engineering firm, and played for Wanderers RFC one of the top rugby clubs in the city. Another injury, this time a broken leg, failed to deter him and he recovered to play again before joining another distinguished club, Palmerston.

When his playing days were over, David took his coaching qualifications under the direction of Scotland's national team coach Bill Dickinson and put theory into practice with the junior team at Palmerston for a couple of years. Active participation in sport always remained important to him and in the 1970s he played in goal for Pembroke Wanderers Hockey Club and took up golf. Meanwhile his professional career flourished and in 1977 he was appointed manager of the machine tool section at another Dublin engineering company, Modern Tool Limited. He was still working for them at the time of his death on 25 June 1998.

In 1965 David had married Irene, a hockey international who still works part-time for the Irish Hockey Union. They had three sons, Andrew, Gary and Stuart, all keen sportsmen who, appropriately, have an annual weekend contest among themselves and their friends for the David Johnston Memorial Golf Trophy.

Rhys David Thomas (Neath Grammar School)

Born: 7 June 1937 5'10" 11st 10lb Centre Tour Number: 4

After two seasons in the centre for the Wales' team, the trip to South Africa promised to be a fitting climax to Rhys Thomas' secondary schools' career. An outstanding all round sportsman at Neath Grammar School, he had been a prominent member of a first XV that remained unbeaten in two of the previous three seasons. He had come through the trial matches in the autumn of 1954 to play for the Rest against Wales in the final trial at Abertillery and then win his first cap against the touring South African High Schools in Newport. He continued in the side against France and England and in 1956 played again against Yorkshire and England. He was always likely to be busy in South Africa and so it proved, with selection for five of the eight games.

Rhys Thomas crashes over for the first try of the game against Transvaal.

Rhys was an able linguist, a skill that several of his team-mates, not least John Elgar Williams, had good cause to be particularly grateful for on the voyage home. As John Elgar explains, 'We stopped off at Las Palmas in the Canary Islands and it was a piping hot day. As we strolled around with our shirts off I was suddenly thumped from behind by a local policeman. He was jabbering away in Spanish and I didn't have a clue what he was going on about. Luckily, Rhys was with us, could speak the language and sorted out the problem – it was an offence to go around topless! Thanks to him I reckon I narrowly escaped a couple of hours in the local cooler'.

Rhys' mastery of languages continued to be put to good use in his teaching career. But first of all on his return home, he went off to complete his National Service in the army and then in 1958 he began his teacher training at St Luke's College in Exeter. He had already played a few games of senior rugby for Swansea and Penarth and he now began his long association with the Neath club, playing for St Luke's during term time and for the Welsh All Blacks during college vacations. Once he had qualified and began his teaching career at Seven Sisters Comprehensive School, he became a Neath regular, was appointed vice-captain at the Gnoll in 1964-65, and the following season took over the captaincy from the international full back, Grahame Hodgson.

In later years he was a mainstay at Crynant RFC, combining committee work with coaching. After two years at Seven Sisters, he taught at Cwrt Sart Comprehensive where he was appointed a head of year. Rhys retired in 1994 and was a very keen golfer at Neath Golf Club where he also captained the veterans' team. He died on 12 January 2003 after a long illness leaving a widow, Mary.

Trevor Edward Evans (Caerphilly Grammar School)

Born: 6 October 1938 5'9" 11st 10lb Wing Tour Number: 5

Like all good wings, Trevor Evans had made a late run on the outside to secure his place on the tour. He had won his first cap a few months before, against France at Cardiff Arms Park, a cause for double celebration as at the same time he was confirmed as Young Dragon as well. He says that he considers himself lucky to go on the tour but the selectors had no doubts about his merits and the results and performances during the summer justified their faith. Though one of the youngest members of the party, Trevor played in six games in South Africa, including the first four and then the showpiece fixture against Transvaal. The conditions suited his style of play. He says, 'It was incredibly dry, of course, and it was a classic case of hard and fast rugby. But when you took a knock and went down you hit the ground much harder, too – there was no cushion effect as we were used to in the soft pitches at home.' Trevor, when not in possession himself, was noted for his harrying of opponents. Though the first game in Port Elizabeth was lost, he impressed onlookers with his role in both Welsh tries, making the first for Allan Williams when, it was reported, he 'caught the Eastern Province right wing in possession [and] whipped the ball out to Williams for the wing-forward to race 25 yards down the touchline to score in the corner.' Towards the end of the game Clive Rowlands scored the second try after a thrilling counter-attack when 'Evans received the ball inside his own half and sidestepped his way infield and, when confronted by de Beer, passed to Rowlands who scored in the corner.'

Trevor put his own name on the score sheet a week later at Ermelo, scoring tries either side of half-time as the Young Dragons overwhelmed the Eastern Transvaal Country XV with an exhibition of sparkling rugby. By then, he was more relaxed about the whole experience of being a rugby tourist in a far-off land. He says, 'In some respects I think I didn't make as much of the tour as I should have. Perhaps I was simply too young, but on the other hand there was so much to see and take in. Even simple things like the oranges we were picking in a citrus orchard or the sheer beauty and warmth of the sea in Port Elizabeth in the middle of their winter.'

Trevor returned home with clear academic and career ambitions. Two

Trevor Evans scores the first of his two tries against Eastern Transvaal at Ermelo.

more years in the sixth form at school went hand in hand with further games for the Welsh Secondary Schools, including the captaincy against Yorkshire in 1957, and three further caps, though he was unfortunate to withdraw on the morning of that season's match against England after being injured in a school match against Porth Grammar School. Unusually for a wing he also liked to play at wing-forward, and did so at every opportunity for his school and even for Glamorgan Schools against London, one of the most prestigious fixtures on the representative calendar. In the autumn of 1958 Trevor went to Oxford University, playing occasionally for the first XV and regularly for his college, St Edmund Hall. Though he didn't gain a rugby Blue he also excelled at athletics and was selected for the pole vault in the Varsity Match at the White City Stadium. He had also represented the Welsh AAAs at domestic meetings, though modestly refutes suggestions that he had real potential in the sport. 'I never used a fibre-glass pole and never vaulted higher than 12 feet', he says. As few British pole-vaulters exceeded 13 feet at that time, Trevor was far more proficient than he is prepared to admit.

After Oxford, Trevor went to teach in the statistics department at Aberdeen University for 13 years, losing touch with rugby but still receiving plenty of exercise with hill walking, climbing and cycle touring. A keen orienteer, he was also a member of the Aberdeen mountain rescue team. In 1976, he returned south and taught mathematics at Millfield School in Somerset, a renowned centre of sporting as well as academic excellence. He still lives nearby and answers the call for supply teaching from time to time.

Alan Morgan Henry Rees (Glan Afan Grammar School, Port Talbot)
Born 17 February 1938 5'6" 10st 8lb Fly Half Tour Number: 6

Alan Rees was always going to be a great favourite with the South African rugby cognoscenti. All the Young Dragons travelled in the wake of the successful British Isles' tour of 12 months earlier but Alan and his fellow fly-halves Dewi Robinson and Ieuan Jones were earmarked to receive extra attention. At every turn they were compared to the charismatic Cliff Morgan. Modern players might consider that an unwanted burden but for Alan, at least, it was something he regarded as a compliment.

He said, 'For all Welsh youngsters Cliff was regarded as an icon. There was no way that I was in his class but at 18 years of age it was, to say the least, flattering to have the spotlight on me in that way.'

Though he is far too self-effacing to admit it, Alan didn't disappoint his new audiences as he put in a series of impressive performances in five of the first six matches. Local match reports were never slow to draw the predictable conclusions about him being an 'archetypal Welsh fly-half' but they had plenty of evidence on which to base their praise. Typically, after the resounding victory over the Eastern Transvaal Country XV in the third match, it was reported that 'Seven of the eight tries were scored by the fast backline and were mainly due to their outstanding fly-half, Alan Rees.' And later he was again singled out after the 21-3 triumph against Transvaal with the sobriquet that 'he was not unlike the great Cliff Morgan in style'.

The great win at Ellis Park was to coincide with Alan's last appearance on the tour, a leg injury sustained early in the game eventually making him unavailable for the final two matches. But he had played his part as one of the more experienced members of the side to the full. It was a fine end to a distinguished secondary schools' career that had began nearly two years previously as a centre ('But I was never a centre') for Wales against the South African High Schools at Newport. Whatever his critical self-assessment of his abilities further out in the midfield, he was good enough to continue in the role alongside Rhys Thomas with Dewi Robinson at pivot for the next match of 1955 against France in Toulon before reverting to fly-half against England in Cardiff. By the start of the 1956 campaign he was also chosen as captain against Yorkshire before the role was handed to David Walkey.

Send-offs were always important and the neighbourhood is out in force before Alan Rees departs for South Africa.

His selection for the tour was never in doubt. As with the majority of his team-mates he received a suitable send-off with the presentation of a travelling clock from his neighbours in Richard Street, Port Talbot. A stand had already been taken by his father against the practice of means-testing by the Glamorgan Education Authority to assess his eligibility for the £25 LEA grant, a proud decision that eventually ended happily for all concerned. In playing terms, Alan brought the vital extra ingredient of experience to the Young Dragons. He had already dipped his toes into county cricket for Glamorgan, making his first-class debut as a seventeen-year-old against Somerset at Weston-super-Mare in 1955. In later years he was to establish a reputation as one of the finest cover point fielders on the county circuit. His 216 matches included Glamorgan's historic victories of the touring Australians in 1964 and 1968.

But as the Young Dragons returned home in the early autumn of 1956 Alan's rugby career still had many landmarks awaiting. First of all, though, there was two years' National Service awaiting him in the RAF. Several of his fellow Young Dragons were rarely far away, notably the ubiquitous D C T Rowlands. Alan and Clive were destined to become senior internationals for Wales, though missing a half-back partnership together by one year. Alan was to win his three caps in 1962; Clive began his three-year stint at scrum-half in 1963. Back in 1956 their daily life in the RAF was what Alan playfully describes as more like a master and servant relationship.

With a twinkle in his eye he recalled, 'I was Rowlands' batman! The situation hadn't changed from what happened in South Africa when he always blamed me for being responsible for his fractured collar-bone against Orange Free State. After that, he was always playing the old soldier and I was forever fetching and carrying for him. You can imagine how pleased I was to now find myself with him in the RAF at Hednesford. In the barracks I was virtually providing a bed and breakfast service for him – and then we both got transferred to Yorksbury in Wiltshire and it still continued!'

Regular rugby helped Alan to survive his Jeeves-like role in uniform. Officially he was a radar mechanic; in reality he had a whale of a time playing twice a week for the RAF against the top club sides of England and Wales. When the opportunities arose, he also turned out for Aberavon, Maesteg and Llanelli. A prospective half-back partnership at Stradey Park alongside Onllwyn Brace looked particularly attractive but never quite materialised. Ironically, the next generation of gifted secondary schools' backs, D Ken Jones and Brian Davies, were also about to try their luck there. Wanting regular first class rugby, Alan went back to Maesteg and from there into the full Wales side. He was an ever-present throughout the 1962 Five Nations matches though the game against Ireland was postponed because of a smallpox outbreak in South Wales.

His biggest regret of that period is that he didn't make himself available for the 1962 British Isles tour to South Africa. He may or may not have been selected but we shall never know. Instead he played another summer of county cricket for Glamorgan and at the end of it began what was to be a brief rugby league career with Leeds.

'I was up there for three years,' he said, 'but things never quite worked out as planned. At first it seemed a good arrangement – rugby league from September to April with a built-in agreement for me to return to the cricket every spring.'

The balancing of two first-class sporting careers finally ended after a match against Featherstone Rovers. 'I was swung around in a tackle and had a knee injury that was never really sorted. Years later I was still getting aches and pains from it. I soon realised that it was the beginning of arthritis.'

In the years since, Alan has never been far away from active sport. His first-class cricketing days ended in 1968 but at various times he has played Welsh League soccer for Afan Lido ('I was a tricky outside-right'), a county player in badminton, and a squash representative for Wales Veterans. He still lives in Port Talbot, where for many years he was deputy sports officer for the local council. To cap it all, he has taken up golf in recent years and, as always, is competitive out on the course.

Howard Francis Merrick (Cathays High School, Cardiff)

Born: 11 August 1937 5'8" 11st 6lb Scrum-Half Tour Number: 7

From the *Arundel Castle* to Arizona may seem an unusual journey, but that is the route that Howard Merrick's life has taken since he became a Young Dragon in 1956. En route, the former Cathays High School student from Cardiff has stopped off at his local university, then Cambridge, New York State and several points west across the United States. It has been quite an adventure for a young rugby player who, like so many of his contemporaries, has balanced any ambitions based on his sporting prowess with the equally important priority of furthering his academic and professional career.

At the start, Howard went to South Africa as the most experienced, and therefore first-choice, scrum-half. He had had to bide his time before attaining that status. Scrum-half was one of the most competitive positions in the side even before the tour was first mooted. In 1955, another Cardiff schoolboy, the mercurial Leo Karseras had been a fixture in the position for both Cardiff Schools and Wales but by 1956 Howard had taken over for city, where he was also team captain, and country. He had won his first cap against Yorkshire and also played against England at Gloucester. The French game had been an opportunity for Maurice Palmer to press his claims and when the tour party was announced the secondary schools' selectors followed the example set by the Lions a year before and accommodated three scrum-halves in the 28-man squad – Howard, Maurice and Clive Rowlands. There was every prospect that competition for the position promised to be as keen in South Africa as it had been at home. On tour, the selectors were extremely fair: Howard played in the first game, Clive the second, and Maurice the third. But the unfortunate injury suffered by Clive Rowlands at Bloemfontein, immediately took him out of the future equation.

Howard has many memories of his month in South Africa with even the long railway journeys failing to disrupt his enjoyment. He says: 'On the two-night train ride to Port Elizabeth five of us – Dave Walkey, Clive Phillips, Malcolm Thomas, Neville Johnson and myself – played solo whist for 10 hours, in commemoration of which we signed the aces! And wherever we went we were put up in the homes of people who were generously supporting the tour. My first one in Port Elizabeth was with Tjol Lategan, who toured the UK with the 1951-52 Springboks.'

An unusual memento of the tour. After a marathon game of solo on the long train journey from Cape Town to Port Elizabeth, Howard Merrick's ace of clubs was signed by David Walkey, Clive Phillips, Malcolm Thomas and Nev Johnson.

This touches upon another important aspect of the tour for the Young Dragons: they frequently came into contact with some of the greatest names in Springbok rugby and the encouragement they received from them was priceless. Lategan, for instance, not only toured Europe but in 1949 had been an ever-present in South Africa's midfield in the epic four-match home test series against the All Blacks. His centre partnership with Ryk van Schoor is still considered one of the finest to wear the green and gold jersey.

The generous hospitality and the sights of the vast country also left an impression on Howard. 'We were entertained royally everywhere. Highlights included the barbecue, or braaivleis, which was something totally new to me and probably the other Dragons. The trip to the Kruger Park was also memorable (how I wish I had possessed a digital camera!). This was an all-day adventure and we saw a wide variety of wildlife. In a visit to Pretoria we had the opportunity to view the huge Voortrekker Monument, built as a memorial to those who left the Cape Colony between 1835 and 1838 to found a new state in the northern interior which became Transvaal.'

Clearly there was a strong educational element to the tour, and Howard goes on to say that what he saw in South Africa was fit to compare with many things he has seen since in his much-travelled life. A visit

Howard (second left) sightseeing at Port Elizabeth with Rhys Thomas, Maurice Palmer and Guto Davies

to the Big Hole near the diamond town of Kimberley was fascinating. I have seen the Grand Canyon in Arizona but the Big Hole will be a memory that will stay with me. Deep down you could see water in the hole but I believe its useful days were over. We had a tour of the building where they kept samples of the diamonds – quite amazing'.

The unique structure of South African society also fascinated him. 'The subject of apartheid was to be avoided but it was clearly evident. At the same time there were the little things and incidents that were memorable. In Springs, where we played Eastern Transvaal, a few of us met up with Speedy who was the son of one of our hosts. He had a large car which to me looked like a full size American sedan. He took us for a drive over the Veldt at speeds of at least 100mph!'

Immediately after the tour Howard entered Cardiff University to study science, focusing on materials science. During the first year he played a full season for the University first XV and in 1957 joined the city club, Glamorgan Wanderers. He played for the Wanderers, who had a full fixture list with all the first-class clubs in Wales, for three seasons. Having graduated with first-class honours he went up to Cambridge in October 1960 to do a PhD. Winning a rugby Blue was also a possibility though Howard knew that competition would be keen with the future England scrum-half Simon Clarke also among the contenders. But the rivalry was never tested as Howard suffered a serious knee injury in the trials. His playing career was effectively over. An eminent career in scientific research in both Britain and the United States would prove worthy compensation.

Howard's first three years of research in materials science was under the tutelage of Sir Robin Nicholson before, in 1964, he took up a new post at the International Nickel Company's research centre in Suffern, New York. He also published articles in science journals, was awarded a number of patents, and in 1968 received the Marcus A Grossman Young Authors award for the best paper published in the American Society for Metals scientific journal. In 1980 he received further recognition with an award for one of the ten most significant new technical products of 1980.

Thankfully, Howard's life was not one of all work and no play. Young Dragons' choirmaster Malcolm Thomas would approve of the news that Howard joined the Rockland County Choral Society and he also played what he describes as 'recreational soccer' and took up golf and 'has been hacking away ever since'. Meanwhile, he progressed through several management and research roles in Connecticut, Stratford and eventually Phoenix, Arizona with Honeywell International. He won and managed several government contracts and in 2003 received a Technical Achievement Award for outstanding and innovative contribution in the development of a nickel base super alloy. Phew! To cap a remarkable career, in 2004 he was presented with a Honeywell Aerospace Technology Achievement Award in recognition of technical innovation and accomplishment.

Howard and his wife Ceridwen, originally from Ton Pentre, still live in Arizona. He happily admits to spending more time with their three children and eight grandchildren – but manages to fit in some travelling and golf.

David Gerald Alan Walkey (Bassaleg Grammar School)
Born 29 November 1937 5'10" 13st 7lb Prop/Lock Tour Number: 8

The captaincy was in safe hands following the appointment of David Walkey. The term 'natural leader' can be an overused cliché but in his case it was entirely appropriate. He had led the Newport Schoolboys' team at under-15 level and at Bassaleg he was rugby captain for three years and Head Boy for two. He was also a fine all-round sportsman having excelled at sprinting to such an extent that by the time of the tour he was already the Wales Schools' 100 yards champion with the remarkable time of 10.2 seconds; a year later in the RAF he lowered that personal best to 10 seconds exactly. Little wonder that his fellow Young Dragon, John Elgar Williams, described his play at prop as revolutionary for the era.

In fact David was equally comfortable in any row of the pack. Three years earlier he had won under-15 caps at both prop and second row (the latter when Nev Johnson and Howell Morgan filled the front row berths) and midway through the South African trek he switched from prop to the middle of the back row. Wherever he played he was exceptional for his age. After the tough battle against Orange Free State one South African newspaper reported: 'Skipper David Walkey of Bassaleg reminds us of Bryn Meredith, the Lions hooker who earned such a high reputation for intelligent and zealous work in the loose.' Interestingly, the legendary Meredith began his senior career as a prop, went on to become a world-class hooker, and on the second of his three Lions' tours turned out at wing forward in one match in Australia in 1959.

David never quite achieved that eminence in senior rugby (few players of any generation do) but he left a lasting legacy at the helm of the Young Dragons. He was equally as effective off the field as on it. Everyone testifies to his remarkable maturity as a public speaker and in fulfilling the ambassadorial role. He admits that he never found such responsibilities, ones that other captains might regard as onerous tasks, tiresome and usually relished them. That may be partly down to the fact that he was one of the oldest players in the team. He amusingly reveals, 'I had already completed my third year in the sixth form at Bassaleg and, frankly, it was a very satisfactory situation. I had taken most of my 'A' Levels when I was 17 and by the time I entered my third year I only had chemistry to sit. Little school work needed to be done.'

He also admits that the ethos at Bassaleg was the perfect preparation for the captaincy role. 'The way we were encouraged by the school to take responsibility for our actions stood me in good stead for my profile on the tour.' Certainly even comparative strangers recognised him as a figure of authority. 'On the voyage out on the *Arundel Castle* the chaperon of one group of girls on the ship approached me and said, "You will keep your boys in order, won't you?"!'

David Walkey is chaired off by his opponents after the first game at Port Elizabeth.

Testimony from his team mates suggests that he did just that, or at least followed the classic diplomatic approach from time to time of 'hear no evil, see no evil'...Whatever the intention, they all still regard David as the ideal choice as their spokesman and figurehead. He set a fine example and, as one of them, explained, 'We all looked up to him'. There was much to admire. For a start, he played in all eight games, as indeed did Brynle Harrison. He does admit that towards the end of the tour he was beginning to feel weary but by then his Young Dragons had left their mark. He says, 'After the disappointing result in the opening game at Port Elizabeth, our performance against the Orange Free State was the turning point of the tour. Going into that game we felt up against it. They were a massive team but we played very well. Crucially, we were much more mobile than they were and even though we were reduced to 14 men after Clive Rowlands' injury we were ahead until the dying moments. It ended as a draw but for us it was a case of coming through a harsh trial with a moral victory.'

David frankly reflects that the team surprised itself with the big win at Ellis Park a fortnight later and by the time the penultimate match at Kimberley was also won fatigue was really setting in. He adds, 'After beating the Griquas we were very tired and looking forward to the finish of the tour. There had also been talk of us fulfilling an extra fixture against a representative South African XV but that was never going to happen at such a late stage. Such a match would have to be pre-planned long before the tour started and then we could have built up properly to a fitting climax. I suspect the truth is that by the time we had strung our winning run together the South Africans didn't like to see their teams being beaten!'

On his return home David was another of the Young Dragons to immediately begin his National Service in the RAF. Over the course of the next two years he was successively stationed at Cardington, Hednesford, Hereford and Innsworth before resuming his studies at Cardiff University in 1958. He had already tasted senior club rugby with Newport though he admits he regrets not trying to switch to hooker whilst there. He then had a successful three seasons with Penarth, also captained the Welsh Universities, and in 1961 tried his luck with Cardiff. In two seasons at the Arms Park he played over 40 times for the Athletic XV but his time and his priorities were already being delicately balanced between sport and his academic and professional ambitions.

Having completed his degree in zoology and botany, David then went on to take a PhD, specialising in the study of fungal diseases. This was the launch pad to an eminent career at Wellesbourne where he became deeply involved in the research of plant viruses. Apart from a year spent in Canada in 1971-2 he remained attached to Wellesbourne until he took early retirement in 1993. He still lives near there in south Warwickshire. He had been as successful as a scientist as he had been as a leader of the Dragons all those years earlier. And for him, the two experiences were inter-connected.

'The tour to South Africa changed my life. I became more aware of personal responsibilities, the value of achievements, and the importance of character-building. I came away from it with more self-confidence and it all stood me in good stead for later years when I was speaking at scientific conferences and dealing with all sorts of unforeseen issues. I will never forget the lessons of those two months in 1956.'

David John Jones (Mountain Ash Grammar School)
Born 5 April 1938 5'9" 12st 7lb Hooker Tour Number: 9

Dai Jones proved to be one of the great work horses of the pack, playing in seven matches in South Africa and only missing the game at Springs against Eastern Transvaal. For him, it really was a case of grasping his opportunities with both hands. For a long time he thought that he would miss out on the tour. Disappointment and near-misses had been regular bedfellows in his schoolboy rugby career. A mainstay of the redoubtable Mountain Ash school team that regularly supplied youngsters to representative selections, at under-15 level he had travelled the length and breadth of South Wales to play in the exhaustive yet protracted trial matches that led to the selection of the Wales' Schools sides that annually played the South of Scotland and then England home and away. The nearest he came to the cherished scarlet jersey was a reserve card on no less than three occasions in 1954. In the sides that actually took the field that spring were future Young Dragons David Walkey, Nev Johnson and Howell Morgan.

As the road to South Africa beckoned two years later, he could be forgiven for thinking that he was also about to be overlooked at Welsh Secondary Schools level. A Bassaleg School team-mate of David Walkey, David Williams, received the nod for the opening game of the 1956 international season against Yorkshire. But then Dai's fortunes changed. He won his cap against France at Cardiff Arms Park and a fortnight later packed down again against England at Gloucester. After that he went from strength to strength.

'The only problem was,' he smiled ruefully, 'that I played so many games in South Africa that it took a heavy toll on my back. I wasn't complaining because once I had got into the side every game was something to treasure. The opposition front rows were tough, particularly in the Free State, but they were nothing we couldn't handle. We were particularly strong at prop and could even afford to move David Walkey to the back row for the second half of the tour. Malcolm Thomas, Nev Johnson and Howell Morgan were all good scrummagers.'

Dai Jones is ready for whatever is coming as the *Arundel Castle* Crosses the Line!

Dai will admit that the opening game at Port Elizabeth proved to be a tough baptism – he even concedes that he lost the tight-head count 2-1 to his opposite number, Rob Mundell, a future Currie Cup player – but insists that the Young Dragons were never disconcerted by the focused scrummaging of the locals wherever they went.

'I never felt anything until we were on the voyage home. Then, with the excitement of the tour beginning to die down, the aches and pains kicked in. I was literally shuffling around the ship rather than walking in the final fortnight.'

On his return home he went back to school for his scholarship year in the sixth form. As his back recovered and kept him out of the game for several months he was able to concentrate on his studies and entered Aberystwyth University in the autumn of 1957. Now he could put his boots on again and found himself in the same team as Jack Davies. 'Aber' were a useful side, reaching the UAU Final before losing to the mighty Loughborough Colleges. He also played half-a-season for Llanelli but at a cost. Not this time his back, but too little time in the lecture rooms resulted in less than satisfactory examination marks and a year out from his studies.

Like all true hookers, young Dai was prepared to take the rough with the smooth. He went home to Mountain Ash and worked in Treforest for a year as a fitter's mate. Rugby remained on his agenda and he played the first of his two seasons at Newbridge, this time with yet another Young Dragon, Dewi Jones, before resuming his studies in Aberystwyth. His second coming was more successful than the first both on and off the field. John Dawes was rugby captain and Dai his deputy as the team again reached the UAU Final. His regular appearances for Newbridge also helped his selection for Monmouthshire, in the counties' championship, and the Welsh Academicals.

In 1962 Dai's playing activities were put on the back burner for a second time. Having taken a teaching diploma in his final year at university, his appointment to the staff of King's School, Macclesfield, understandably took centre-stage in his life.

'This was a career opportunity I really valued and I was given responsibility for developing the rugby teams at the school. I loved every minute of it and I like to think that I helped to mould a very positive sporting culture there.'

Few students or staff who benefited from Mr Jones' teaching at the school would dispute that. He stayed for 36 years, working his way up the profession to become Senior Master and a mentor to countless rugby players, including future England and Lions' scrum-half, Steve Smith. Many of the lessons he had learnt as a Young Dragon in South Africa were put into practice. One such initiative was his insistence on regular tours by the school team.

'We were ambassadors for the school and we travelled everywhere, from my old hunting grounds in Wales to the south of France and throughout Europe.' With a sense of mischief he reveals that he even arranged home and away fixtures with a school team in Chile – both played within the space of a fortnight!

His own playing days had concluded with a few games for the local Macclesfield club, where he also helped to introduce mini-rugby, and his coaching extended to Cheshire Schools. In 1998 he retired and now keeps a watching brief on the ever-changing scene in first-class rugby in Wales from the new family home in Cefn Cribwr.

Malcolm Howard Henry Thomas (Tonyrefail Grammar School)
Born 3 January 1938 5'11" 15st 0lb Prop Tour Number: 10

The great adventure to South Africa in 1956 obviously provided Malcolm Thomas with a wanderlust that has become a feature of his life over the past half-century. Five years after he returned home with the Young Dragons he was on his travels again. He first moved to New Zealand, then returned to Wales for a short while, and then spent some time working and playing in Australia, before finally settling in New Zealand where he still lives. Before all that happened, though, he left his mark on South Africa in at least two ways: he was a durable, no nonsense prop – and he was the team's choirmaster. The latter, if anything, was the more significant because, as everyone agrees, the choral singing, impromptu or otherwise before or after matches, or on railway station platforms, or school halls, in fact anywhere, became one of the most distinctive and best-loved memories of the entire tour.

David Walkey remembers one occasion when on a school visit Malcolm Pemberton and himself, a self-confessed tone-deaf baritone, narrowly escaped what he feared would be the ultimate embarrassment of a duet in front of a class of expectant pupils by frantically sending for reinforcements in the shape of Malcolm and his more melodic choristers. Welsh musical reputations were upheld with the captain mercifully taking up his permanent semi-miming position in the back row. Malcolm Thomas, though, was undeniably of the front rank both on and off the pitch.

Yet he seems to have been, initially at least, a reluctant conductor. He says, 'I have no idea why the job fell to me. I had never studied music and there *must* have been someone in our group who had – but no one else volunteered.' It was a responsibility that Malcolm took seriously. 'We practised on the ship going out and we were lucky enough to have someone, a woman I think, teach us *Sarie Marais*, a lovely Afrikaaner song that became one of our party pieces.' He thought right. In fact the lady in question was a very accomplished teacher of music returning home. Malcolm was not short of other reliable help, too. He continues: 'From school I knew that Edwin 'Ned' Gribble (always '*Mr*' Gribble to me) had a bass voice to balance a throng and knew the bass part and so there would be at least some harmony. As it turned out there were others who could also harmonise and so the sound reaching me was pleasant enough.' From such promising beginnings a fine Young Dragons' choir took shape.

Malcolm was a pretty useful rugby player as well. He was First XV captain at Tonyrefail School and had played in all three international matches of the 1956 season. On tour he was to be equally prominent, appearing in the last five games. After the tour he turned out for his local Tonyrefail club team while studying mathematics and physics at Cardiff University. When he moved to New Zealand in 1961 he joined the Pukekohe Rugby Club and also represented the Counties provincial team on half-a-dozen occasions. By 1964 he was back in Wales and represented Seven Sisters in the West Wales League, no place for shrinking violets at the best of times. His personal odyssey was far from finished, however, because his next port of call was Ballarat in Australia. 'As there was no rugby union being played in that part of Victoria I became a half-back flanker in Aussie Rules. Eventually I moved to Sydney and looked forward to playing for the Gordon club in 1967. But I picked up a bad

eye injury in the final pre-season practice match so I decided that my eyesight was more important to me than playing rugby so that was the end of my playing career.'

It was, though, far from the end of Malcolm's involvement with rugby. Over the years (and around the world) he has coached teams at every school he has taught at – 'All told this comes to about twenty different teams, including five First XVs.' His sporting activities have also extended to tennis, badminton and soccer but chiefly squash and now croquet. He says he intends playing the latter 'until I die'. Fellow members of the 1956 front row union would indeed relish the image of the prop forward hewn from solid Welsh foundations in Tonyrefail now being the demon of the croquet lawn in New Zealand. He must be doing so pretty well as he proudly points out that he represents Waikato province at croquet.

As he does so, his mind must surely drift back to that historic summer of 1956. He admits, 'Certain incidents and events will

Old props don't retire...they become champion croquet players. Malcolm Thomas at play in New Zealand.

always stand out. There was the silver service dining car on our 39-hour train journey from Cape Town to Port Elizabeth, the massive party at the Springs gold mine (which just happened to have a Welsh manager), and wherever we went the magnificent hospitality. Most of all, of course, there was the singing. Whenever we congregated as a group we were expected to sing for our hosts and they were always appreciative. We actually made three radio broadcasts during the tour.'

These days Malcolm is still living in New Zealand. He retired from teaching mathematics and physics at the age of 55. Education's loss has been croquet's gain!

Brynle Harrison (Grove Park School, Wrexham)

Born: 6 May 1937 6'1" 13st 5lb Second Row Tour Number: 11

Like David Johnston, Bryn Harrison was a proud representative of North Wales rugby among the Young Dragons. Indeed, he was only the second student from Grove Park School in Wrexham to be selected for the national side. A year earlier Bryan Woolley, a speedy wing and long jumper, had been its first capped player against Yorkshire, the South African High Schools and France. Bryn played twice during the 1956 international season at home but, more remarkably, in South Africa shared the distinction with his skipper David Walkey of appearing in all eight matches – and scoring three tries for good measure.

Spotting rugby talent in the north was not always straightforward for the largely southern based selectors. The comprehensive trials' system helped but in the case of someone like Bryn, the cream was always going to rise to the top. He played four seasons in his school's first XV, won his colours at the tender age of 15, and eventually became captain; he also led the North Wales regional team in representative matches and trials. As his potential was recognised, long journeys south by road or rail became the norm during the winter months. They were not without their brighter moments, as when David Johnston and himself were changing trains one day at Shrewsbury.

He recalls, 'David was in his cadets' uniform from HMS Conway and while we were waiting on the platform an old girl went up to him and asked him to carry her bags – she thought he was a porter!'

The serious side of the trips were also memorable as Bryn got to know many of his future Young Dragons team-mates quite well. 'That was important to me, firstly when I was selected to play against Yorkshire and England and, as luck would have it, when I had the great honour to be picked to go to South Africa. If everyone had been strangers to me at the outset it would have been a much more daunting prospect.'

Others also regarded Bryn's selection as an honour for his town and his school. The usual pre-tour presentations followed: a holdall and other accessories from Wrexham Rugby Club and a much-valued achievement award from his school. Bryn was determined to soak up everything from the tour and to enjoy it. Even before the team left Wales he knew he was part of something special. He explains, 'Just being in a weekend training camp at St Athan and in the company of legends like Cliff Morgan, Russell Robins and the rest was a big thing for me. And there was a day at Newport Station when Malcolm Pemberton introduced me to the great wing, Ken Jones. These were stars that I had only read about, now I was not only seeing them in the flesh but being introduced to them as well.'

The voyage out contained one disappointment for Bryn. Rather quirkily, he was looking forward to some rough seas in the Bay of Biscay. He says, 'Compared to what I was expecting, it was rather calm and I felt really let down!'. Others among the team would disagree – at least a dozen were reported to be seasick. Bryn, though, admits to being nervous once in South Africa as the first match approached. 'After months of waiting and thinking about it, we were suddenly in Port Elizabeth and it was all about to happen. I won't deny that I was edgy ahead of the game against Eastern Province.'

The nerves proved beneficial. Though the team lost for the only time on the tour, Bryn overcame the handicap of losing his second row partner Jack Davies to injury and made a big impression in a depleted pack. 'He is someone we will be hearing a lot more of,' opined one local scribe. They did.

As the tour progressed, Bryn became more and more prominent and he was enjoying every minute of it. He says, 'The South Africans were the biggest forwards I or anyone else had ever played against but we did well. I was comparatively light and mobile and the hard grounds suited us. By the time the first five games had been played and we had won three in a row I was really looking forward to taking on Transvaal at Ellis Park.' The records show that it was not a misplaced confidence on his part. He scored two tries in the 21-3 win and went on to complete a full house of appearances at Kimberley and Wellington.

However, he admits to sharing his team-mates' concerns about the divided nature of South African society. He says, 'What apartheid entailed is now well- documented. For us in 1956 it was a real shock to the system and I didn't like it one bit. Here we were, staying in large, comfortable homes and being offered lavish hospitality but the blacks were not allowed to sleep under the same roof as us. There was one exception, of sorts, though, when at one home in the Transvaal I was billeted in a shed at the bottom of the garden. Having seen what I had seen elsewhere, including the segregation on public transport, I had no intention of complaining. I think it did me good.'

Nevertheless, Bryn appreciated the beautiful scenery, first viewed on the long train ride from Cape Town to Port Elizabeth, and the wildlife in the Kruger National Park, and he returned home better and wiser for the whole experience. His father was a farmer and he had long harboured an ambition to become a vet. So off he went to the Royal Veterinary College at London University for five years of hard study with just a bit of rugby thrown in. The exiles' grapevine, always on the lookout for new talent in town, had reached London Welsh and he was invited to play for them. It was an attractive prospect but proved a difficult decision to make. He explains, 'Scouts from London Welsh had come to see me play college rugby but my first loyalty had to be to continue playing for the college. However, I was able to go with the Exiles on their tour to South Wales during the Christmas

Bryn Harrison, ever-present Young Dragon in eight matches, survived to become a successful vet in Wrexham.

vacation of 1956. I thoroughly enjoyed the experience, playing in three matches against Neath, Llanelli and in the unfamiliar position of prop against Swansea. In some ways I regret I didn't play for them regularly.'

Bryn also played county games for Hertfordshire but unfortunately his playing career came to a sudden halt at the start of the next season when he broke a leg while playing for the university. He rationalises any initial disappointment by concluding, 'In many ways it was a blessing in disguise because with no rugby to play for several months I was able to knuckle down to my studies and make sure I qualified as a vet.' In September 1961 he returned to Wrexham and joined a five-man practice, became a partner in 1967 and by 1974 was senior partner of what had mushroomed into a practice of 13 vets. Bryn retired in 1997 and quietly admits to watching Sale Sharks on a regular basis but balances that with the traditional 'Welsh weekends' at Six Nations' matches around the British Isles and Europe.

David John Puddle (Brynmawr Grammar School)

Born: 23 March 1938 5'11" 14st 0lb Second Row Tour Number: 12

John Puddle was regarded as one of the 'quiet men' of the tour. He came from the same school as one of its driving forces, T Rowley Jones, a fact that made the teacher doubly proud of his pupil playing his way through the trials and proving his worth as both an international player and a Young Dragon.

John was a powerful scrummager and also mobile in loose play, making him equally adept in the front and second row of the pack. In February 1955 he had been selected as a second rower alongside the future Lion and Wales' captain Alun Pask in the Monmouthshire team that played the touring South African High Schools. A year later he made his international debut against England at Gloucester, the last game before the Young Dragons left for South Africa. On the tour he made one appearance, again as a second row, in the penultimate fixture against Griqualand West at Kimberley. He returned to Brynmawr Grammar School and a further international cap followed in 1957, again against England, when he played at prop.

After leaving school John attended Swansea University for one year before transferring to Newland Park College in Chalfont St Giles where he studied French and geography. Whilst there he also played for the college's first XV and in later years after his return to South Wales he played for several local teams, including Tredegar and Blaenavon. His first teaching appointment was in

John Puddle played for the Welsh Secondary Schools against England both before and after the tour.

Bristol, then he moved to Tredegar and also took an Open University degree. In due course John moved again, this time to Nantyglo Comprehensive School where he taught economics and also gave distinguished service to the local council in Brynmawr, where he became mayor, and as a rotarian.

John retired early because of ill-health. He died on 12 December 2000 at the age of 63 and is survived by his widow, Rosamond.

William Thomas Allan Williams (Queen Elizabeth Grammar School, Carmarthen)

Born: 22 October 1937 5'10" 12st 6lb Wing-Forward Tour Number: 13

No rugby tour would be complete without at least one player suffering some form of domestic or organisational mishap involving lost kit, temporary amnesia when trying to remember the whereabouts of the team hotel in the small hours, or finding only one shoe (or worse) to put on in the cold light of dawn. As the Young Dragons prepared to leave Cardiff on the morning of Thursday 19 July 1956, a day that would culminate in them embarking on the *Arundel Castle* for the true beginning of their great adventure, the prospective fall guy turned out to be Allan Williams. It was nothing trivial, either. Young Allan discovered that he had forgotten his passport. Or to be more precise, as he now half admits half a century later, 'It never really occurred to me that I might need it.' Whatever the background, it must have been quite a scene of panic as it suddenly dawned on him as he awoke on that final morning that a vital piece of documentation was missing. As Gwynfor Davies, who taught Allan at Queen Elizabeth Grammar School noted in his tour journal, 'He could have forgotten his rugby kit, his clothes, his money – but not his passport; but he did!'

Allan Williams had already won seven caps for the Welsh Secondary Schools before he became a Young Dragon.

Allan takes up the story: 'I had stayed the night before with one of the team near Neath but I suddenly realised at breakfast time that I had forgotten my passport. We were due to assemble in Cardiff the next day in readiness for the last lap of the journey to Southampton. So I suppose it could have been a lot worse. My mother would only have to bring the passport from West Wales to Cardiff. The trouble was that she wasn't on the telephone – hardly anybody was in 1956 – so we had to contact the local telephone exchange and from there the police were involved in passing on the message to her. I suppose there must have been quite a commotion in Kidwelly when all this was going on but Ma was great. She caught the first train to Cardiff and brought me my passport.'

Panic over – well, not quite. The other 27 players and six teachers had long since departed for the south coast by the time passport and Dragon were reunited so now it was time for Allan to catch the first available train. 'When I eventually reached Southampton the rest of the team had already embarked the ship, which is why I'm not in the photograph of them doing so!' But he made it in good time before the 4.00pm sailing and after such a preamble his day could only get better. It did.

Beforehand, Allan had been regarded as one of the automatic choices for the team and it was an expectation built on solid foundations. He had been a regular in the Welsh Secondary Schools for two seasons, winning seven caps and generally impressing as a fine all round forward. At school in Carmarthen he had benefited from top-class coaching. As well as Gwynfor Davies he had come under the watchful eye of someone destined to become a legendary figure at international level. He explains, 'Every Thursday afternoon Carwyn James, who was then a young teacher at the school, helped out with our rugby sessions.' Allan had played in the final international trial for the under-15s without playing for Wales but for the secondary schools he was much more successful. He had already added goal-kicking to his armoury and as a flank forward was notably swift around the field. One of his best memories comes from the final international before the tour. 'When we played England at Gloucester they had the Olympic sprinter J R C Young on the wing. He was a real threat and we managed to keep the ball away from him but towards the end of the match he finally received it – and I tackled him from behind!'

After that, surely South Africa's finest young rugby players would hold no fears for Allan. He certainly acquitted himself well once he arrived there. The bare statistics alone show that he was a great success: seven appearances, missing only the penultimate game against Griqualand West and top scorer with 33 points, including two tries and 27 points from the boot. After his first game at Port Elizabeth one newspaper report noted that he was a 'wide awake, dashing flanker' and the commendations continued throughout the following weeks. He admits to

Allan Williams in action against the Free State at Bloemfontein.

thoroughly enjoying the whole experience. 'The games were hard, which was nothing less than we expected. Obviously, things went well for me because I stayed clear of injury and had plenty of games. The highlight, undoubtedly, was at Ellis Park. It was a great thrill to play there, to win, of course, and the icing on the cake for me was that I also managed to score a few points.' In fact he kicked three conversions and a penalty goal in a resounding 21-3 victory.

And, of course, wherever you are in the world you are never far away from Welsh people. Allan recalls, 'We were at a reception with Welsh exiles in the Wanderers club in Johannesburg when a lady approached me and said she had lived next door to my family in Kidwelly years previously. That's what I call some coincidence!'

Immediately after the tour Allan joined the mini-army of Young Dragons who began their National Service. He was one of several who joined the RAF and was stationed for a while at Yatesbury. He later became a mechanic working on Shackletons for Coastal Command at St Mawgan. It was the beginning of a life-long love affair with the delights of Cornwall. He still lives there today in the small town of St Ives. While at St Mawgan he had played for the command team and also in RAF trials and had joined Redruth RFC. In two seasons at the club he missed only one match, ironically against the formidable Welsh outfit of Ebbw Vale. Three more seasons of top-class rugby followed at St Luke's College before he returned across the border to the Duchy. For 14 years he taught PE and mathematics at Bodmin Grammar School and played for St Ives plus one game for the county XV. By the time he hung up his boots in 1970 he was also turning out at full back.

A second teaching stint of 13 years was spent at St Mewan County Primary School in St Austell before he took early retirement at the age of 51. He continued to contribute to the sporting culture of his adopted county and was president of the Cornwall Swimming Association in 1988-89, combining his administrative duties with the coaching of young swimmers.

William Graham Davies (Ebbw Vale Grammar School)
Born 18 March 1938 6'3" 14st 0lb Second Row Tour Number: 14

Graham Davies underwent a significant change in his playing career while in South Africa. Until he became a Young Dragon all his rugby had been played as a number 8 – or lock as the back player of the scrum was known in Britain, at least, at the time. The lineout jumpers were simply the 'second row' and that's exactly what Graham became when he took the field for the first time at Bloemfontein on Saturday 11 August. It was a conversion he took to readily. Against Yorkshire and France in the pre-tour internationals he been in his accustomed role at the back, forming an impressive triumvirate with Allan Williams and Leighton Davies. He heard about his selection for the tour from a distant relative who taught with Rowley Jones at Brynmawr Grammar School, and as expected he was named as a lock. But events in the first week in South Africa conspired to change all the preconceived plans. Jack Davies' dislocated ankle in the opening game against Eastern Province effectively sidelined him for the remaining seven matches. With only two other specialist second rows in the squad – Bryn Harrison and John Puddle – it was decided to try Graham in the position.

The results speak for themselves. After the toughest possible baptism against the Free State forwards, the largest and heaviest pack that would be encountered on the tour, he cemented his place to such an extent that he missed only one more game.

Graham cannot recall whether the Monmouthshire Local Education Authority supported his selection as a Young Dragon with the customary financial grant. What he is sure of is that there was no shortage of well-wishers in his home town. 'Before I left, Ebbw Vale Rugby Club presented me with training kit and on my return the cricket club and the rugby club together awarded me a commemorative gold watch.'

He also made some preparations of his own for the new playing conditions he was about to experience. 'Russell Robins had told us at the weekend camp in St Athan about the hard grounds and their effect on our bodies. His advice, which I readily took, was to rub industrial spirit into my shoulders and joints to harden them up. I did this daily for six weeks before we went.'

Graham Davies (left) and John Puddle looking for more photographic opportunities.

The effort seemed totally worthwhile once he had seen the South African pitches for himself. 'The day before the game at Bloemfontein we went up onto some high ground near the stadium and from a distance the grass looked white. It wasn't quite so alien once I was running out onto it but it was certainly something new in my experience.'

Graham regards that match against the Free State as the best performance of the pack on tour, better even than the celebrated victory at Ellis Park.

'They were very confident that they were going to beat us, particularly as we had lost our first game three days earlier. But we beat them up front and considering we were reduced to 13 men in the closing stages the draw was a significant achievement.'

Another highlight for him were the two days spent in the Kruger National Park, apparently not too concerned by the beasts (of the four-legged variety rather than Young Dragons) that kept him awake at night.

'For me the tour had everything: great rugby, a totally new life experience – and even free ice cream on the ship!'

On his return to Wales Graham wasted no time in getting down to work. Delighted to be newly elected as school rugby captain, he led the team out against Abertillery Grammar School on the morning of Saturday 15 September – barely 24 hours after the *Carnarvon Castle* had docked in Southampton. In his final year at school he would soon have to prove himself all over again to retain his place in the Welsh Secondary Schools' teams for the international matches of 1957. Having played through the trials, he was duly selected to form a new second row partnership with Jack Davies against Yorkshire and England.

In September 1957 Graham entered Cardiff University to study chemistry and also applied to join Cardiff Rugby Football Club. His debut came at very short notice for the Athletic XV in a crunch match against Newport United and so began a distinguished club career for the Blue & Blacks that stretched to 176 first team and 54 Athletic appearances over nine seasons. The highlights included the matches against the Springboks in 1960, a year in which he was also selected for an international trial match, and the All Blacks three years later.

The tempestuous encounter with the Springboks had at least one light hearted postscript. He recalls, 'They had a particularly frightening front row built around an incredible tight-head prop called Piet du Toit. Our loose-head was Colin Howe who had only recently been switched from the other side of the scrum. I told him not to worry because I had seen du Toit with the Dragons in '56 and he was no problem. He was a different du Toit, of course, and Colin is the first to admit that he was put through the mincer.'

Graham also played half a season for Ebbw Vale in 1961-62 and finished his playing career with Bridgend in 1966-67. Then he hung up his boots at the tender age of 28 to concentrate on his teaching career. He had started at Penarth Grammar School in 1961 and eventually became head of science at what became the reorganised Stanwell Comprehensive School before retiring in 1992. He still lives in Penarth.

David Leighton Davies (Garw Grammar School)

Born: 2 June 1938 5'8" 12st 12lb Wing-Forward Tour Number: 15

Leighton Davies fooled everyone when he was forced to pull out at literally the last moment before the opening game of the tour. His sudden illness might have been seen as a portent of all ill-fated few weeks of inactivity to follow. Nothing could have been further from the truth. In fact, missing that curtain-raiser against Eastern Province turned out to be a mere blip on the radar for a dynamic wing forward who from then on barely had time to catch his breath as he played a full part in all of the remaining seven matches.

But back to the events of Port Elizabeth. To no one's surprise Leighton had been selected in an experienced team for the match. He had been the first-choice open-side wing-forward throughout the home season and his mobility and creativity were regarded as important ingredients in the Young Dragons making a favourable first impression in South Africa. But then the surprise element took over. He recalls, 'I was looking forward to the first match tremendously and felt great beforehand. But a few minutes before the kick-off, when I was already changed, I was burning-up. Gwynfor Davies noticed that I was looking flushed so the decision was immediately taken that I should be withdrawn as a precaution – and Clive Rowlands took over at wing-forward.' There has been no shortage of badinage in the years since about the future international scrum-half packing down on the side of the scrum but, as Leighton points out, 'Rowlands ended up wearing my boots in that match and never ran so fast in his life!'

There seem to be no shortage of admirers as Leighton Davies signs autographs after another successful school visit.

Luckily for Leighton, it was only a temporary disappointment as from there his tour went from strength to strength. He was ideally suited to the wing-forward's role, blessed with supreme fitness and the dexterity of the accomplished gymnast that he was. His great friend and deadly modern-day golf rival Jack Davies also describes him as 'a real livewire off the field as well as on it.' By all accounts he was the archetypal bundle of energy and no one was complaining, among the Young Dragons at least, as he made a total nuisance of himself among opposition back divisions. His contribution to the victory over Eastern Transvaal at Springs earned a memorable accolade from South African reporter T J Botha: 'In flanker Davies the Dragons have one of the best schoolboy forwards I have ever seen. As speedy as any of his backs, he completely routed the Easterns' half back combination and was always on hand to link up with his forwards.'

Praise, indeed, but hardly surprising because Leighton was to go on to become one of the finest uncapped, if unluckiest, back row forwards of his generation in Welsh rugby. Yet he came relatively late to the position. His early rugby days at Garw Grammar School were spent at fly-half or, more usually, the centre as he forced his way into the first XV before he reached the sixth form. 'I was reasonably fast so I did alright in the backs but when it came to trials I was no match for the likes of Alan Rees. I was more than happy to be switched to wing-forward eventually.' The move paid off because in 1956 Leighton played in all three internationals against Yorkshire, France and England. There was little doubt that selection for the tour would follow and, when it did, there were the traditional congratulations and presentations from the local club and school. 'Pontycymer Rugby Club gave me a pair of boots and the school presented an inscribed wallet – but unfortunately it was empty. The Garw valley was a typical coal-mining community but both my father and grandfather ran greengrocers' shops so they probably thought, wrongly, that we weren't short of cash!'

Such a misconception failed to cast a shadow over Leighton's excitement at the prospect of the forthcoming trip. 'I knew that when I returned home I would be going straight into National Service. I'd already had the medical and been passed fit and we even had recruiting officers on the train on the way up to Southampton trying to spot the future rugby players for the various services' teams.'

Then there was the peace and quiet of the two weeks' voyage followed by the unforgettable sights as the *Arundel Castle* steamed into Cape Town harbour. 'Seeing Table Mountain from the bay, with the 'tablecloth' half-covering it, was something I couldn't even imagine until I saw it and from there the tour got better and better. Everywhere we went we were treated superbly.'

The successful results gave Leighton particular satisfaction because 'before we went there were people too keen to write us off and it was amusing to see how they had changed their tune by the time we got back.' He had plenty to smile about anyway. His successful performances proved the perfect platform for his future career in senior rugby and that was soon underway. He had joined the RAF and while stationed in the north of England had played for Fylde. The sporting watchdogs in uniform soon spotted his potential and eventually he was transferred to St Athan. The Bridgend club wasn't far away and his debut for them against Pontypool in the 1956-57 season made him the youngest player to be selected for the club. By the spring of 1958 he was deemed good enough to represented a very strong RAF XV in the inter-services' tournament at Twickenham. National Service was followed by two years of college life at St Luke's in Exeter and a year of teacher training back in Cardiff. Thus, he was never far away from top-class rugby.

Appropriately, his first teaching appointment was at Garw Grammar School in 1961 and the following year he took up the post of assistant lecturer at Cardiff Training College. It was the beginning of one of the most distinguished contributions to student rugby in Wales. The college was already benefiting from the presence of some of the pioneering coaches in the game, most notably Roy Bish. A former Welsh Secondary Schools' cap himself, Bish was to eventually coach Cardiff and then the Italian national side. He proved the perfect colleague for Leighton as he cut his teeth in the coaching sphere. For the next ten years he combined his lecturing and coaching at the college with an outstanding playing career for Bridgend. He says, 'It was a good time to be at Bridgend because the club was enjoying one of the most successful periods in its history. Several players, such as Ron Evans, Keith Bradshaw, Ken Richards and John Lloyd, were selected for Wales, and we also won the unofficial Welsh club championship twice and were runners-up on the other two occasions in the space of four years.'

Leighton captained the club to the second of their championships in 1965-66 by which time his selfless service was legendary – in the previous season he had played in 51 of the 52 games and set a club record for a forward of 21 tries. But the elusive senior international cap never quite came. In December 1964 he was selected as part of an all-Bridgend back row, with Gary Prothero and Colin Standing, for an international trial but only Prothero eventually received a call-up to the full Wales' team. In his final year as a player, Leighton accepted an invitation to captain Maesteg and almost repeated a notable double by leading them to the championship. Only three defeats over Easter relegated them to third place; the champions, once again, were Bridgend. But Leighton's connections with both clubs were far from over. At various times in the 1970s and 1980s he coached them, highlighted by the considerable achievement of guiding Maesteg to promotion to the top division of the new Heineken League in 1991. Inevitably, his coaching qualities were recognised in the wider rugby community and he was in a charge of the East Glamorgan team that played the All Blacks at Cardiff Arms Park in 1973, a star-studded Welsh Academicals' squad that toured South Africa in 1981, the President's XV that played Wales in 1984, and the Wales B team that played five matches, including the national XV, in Italy in 1986.

By the time he retired from his lecturing career in 1991, Leighton Davies was generally regarded as one of the best and most influential coaches of his generation. He, in turn, considers himself fortunate to have guided numerous future internationals and recruits to first-class rugby in Wales through their student careers. He lives in Bridgend and still plays a leading role in the activities of the Welsh Academicals' club.

Dewi Treharne Jones (Caerphilly Grammar School)

Born 1 March 1939 5'11" 12st 5lb Full Back Tour Number: 16

Dewi Jones won his first secondary schools' cap a mere five weeks after his 17th birthday in 1956 and three years later he was still playing for Wales. His debut had been against France and he announced his arrival with a touchline conversion of David Johnston's try that sealed a narrow 5-nil victory. The quality of his performance was duly noted because he was to go on to become one of the most dependable full-backs to play for Wales.

Ironically, Dewi's siege-gun goal kicking was not in evidence in South Africa but he was happy to watch the likes of Allan Williams and Ieuan Jones rack up the points. He reflects, 'I was playing in new boots and I didn't like them at all – in fact, when I got home I threw them away!' But his contribution to the success of the tour was significant in every other respect. In raw statistics, he played in six of the matches, impressing South African watchers with the dependability of his defence and, yes, his lengthy touch-kicking. After his debut against Orange Free State local reports commended him for 'never putting a foot wrong'; after the tour-defining victory over Transvaal it was noted that, Jones, their full-back, was always safe. Full marks to him for marking under pressure. So few full-backs do that nowadays'. Dewi has his own particular memory of playing at Ellis Park: 'A high punt was sent into

Dewi Jones saves a certain try against Wales after the ball rebounds from the crossbar at Ellis Park.

our '25' and the ground was so hard and the air so thin that the ball bounced up onto our crossbar. I'd seen nothing like it before!' Understandably, playing at that famous ground and winning so comprehensively remains a highlight of the tour but, commendably for a full-back, he is also full of praise for the pack's play in several matches. 'One that stands out is the game against Western Transvaal. Their forwards had a strong Boer element and we were told in advance that our forwards were in a for a really hard time. In the event it was nothing like that. Our props, Nev [Johnson] and Malcolm [Thomas], really sorted them out.'

Dewi also has particular memories of the enormity of the whole experience of travelling to what seemed like the other side of the world. 'All of us will comment about the fact that we had done very little

Dewi (right) with Bryn Harrison off duty in Bloemfontein

travelling before then. That's well documented. But one of the effects was that for a lot of the time, certainly in the early days, we were very quiet. That definitely applied to the youngest amongst us. There was quite an age difference within the squad. Some of us, like Maurice Palmer, Alwyn Morris and myself, were barely 17, and would be going back to school for two or three years. Others were already 19 and would soon be starting National Service. If anything, we were star struck by the experience of travelling overseas – and also by the realisation that we were representing Wales in a foreign land. And let's remember, no Wales rugby team of any age had travelled further than France before we went to South Africa.'

Equally, Dewi concedes that there was no shortage of strong personalities and extroverts among the group. He describes Nev Johnson and Jack Davies as 'formidable characters' and Clive Rowlands was already showing signs of becoming the charismatic raconteur and humorist of later years. He adds, 'Although there were all sorts of people from different backgrounds the overriding factor in our favour was that we quickly gelled together as a team in every sense of the word. The rooming arrangements and almost daily training on the voyage out and in the first week in South Africa worked brilliantly. David Walkey was also a very sensible choice as captain. There was no doubt that it was the experience of a lifetime – and also lay the foundations for numerous friendships that have lasted and blossomed over the last half-century.'

It certainly gave Dewi and his mates an appetite for the finer things in life. 'The food provided for us has attained a legendary status. Quite apart from all the lunches and dinners we were invited to, we found that there were gifts coming from all directions. A crate full of fresh fruit, such as the grapes that appeared in Cape Town, were typical. We were very sensible most of the time but on the voyage home it was a bit different. There was a waiter on the *Carnarvon Castle* – I think his name was Jim – who looked after us with extra food and even let us have all three desserts on the menu at meal-times. I reckon I put on a stone in weight on the way home – but I was building myself up for the Welsh winter.'

For Dewi, the South African experience was the perfect launch pad for a long and auspicious playing career in schools, college and club rugby. Having been a mainstay of the

Welsh Secondary Schools' team for the next three seasons, finishing with another seven caps, he entered St Luke's College, Exeter in 1959 followed by a teacher training year in Cardiff in 1961. At St Luke's he teamed up again with Leighton Davies, Rhys Thomas and Nev Johnson as the college continued a particularly keen rivalry in annual matches against Cardiff. Then at Cardiff the boot was literally on the other foot as Dewi played in the side that won the home fixture and achieved an honourable draw in the return game at Exeter. During that year at Cardiff Training College Dewi also played a few games for Newport but that was only a forerunner to what was to prove to be a long standing attachment to the Newbridge club. He began a seven-year stint at the Welfare Ground in 1962 and it was a time he thoroughly enjoyed. 'We had a very strong side with Arthur and Dennis Hughes, Ken Braddock and the England number 8 Derek Morgan in the pack, clever half-backs in Elliot Williams and Jeff Palmer, plus John Dawes in the centre. We played some great rugby and were unofficial Welsh club champions in 1965.'

Dewi's own form didn't go unrecognised. He won a Monmouthshire county cap, was reserve for an international trial, and played for the combined Ebbw Vale and Newbridge XV against Canada in 1962. Unfortunately, two years later an injury picked up in a club match against Cross Keys forced him to pull out of another combined team match, for Abertillery and Newbridge, against Fiji. His playing career ended in 1969, by which time he was making notable progress in the business and financial world. Having taught for five years in schools in Glynneath and Ystrad Mynach he had changed course in 1967 and began working for the finance house, Forward Trust. By 1974 he was area manager for the south west of England and a further promotion resulted in him becoming a regional sales executive. He eventually retired after several years with the ANZ Bank and lives in Cardiff from where he continues to survey the rugby scene with a discerning eye and no little exasperation at the vicissitudes of the national game.

David Clive Phillips (Neath Grammar School)
Born: 27 July 1937 5'10" 11st 7lb Wing Tour Number: 17

Clive Phillips was another gifted young player from the great rugby academy at Neath Grammar School. Like Rhys Thomas, he had progressed through the age groups within the school and the Neath Schoolboys' squad that was the next step up. In 1952 he had toured Belgium with the town's under-15 team and his talent continued to be recognised when he became eligible for the senior school team. Another outstanding sportsman at the school was A R Lewis, a future cricket captain of Glamorgan and England and a full back who would eventually win a Cambridge Blue and play first-class rugby for Gloucester and Neath. In his autobiography, *Playing Days*, Tony Lewis revealed how his two schoolboy international team-mates smoothed his path across the Saturday morning pitches of South Wales: 'Rhys was an angelic-looking centre with tumbling fair hair and cherubic lips, but who had the feint, change of pace and swerve of the devil. Clive was the lean greyhound of a wing with sharp Neath Valley knees to knife through any tackles. Floating about between them was a pleasure.'

The 'lean greyhound' soon won honours beyond school and town. In 1955 Clive represented Mid-Glamorgan against the touring South African Schools. The match was played at the Talbot Athletic Ground in Aberavon and attracted a crowd of 5,000. It could hardly be claimed that they were treated to a points scoring feast – the game ended nil-all – but Clive came as close as anyone to breaking the stalemate. With Alan Rees directing operations at fly-half there was no shortage of attacking rugby and reports refer to Clive twice 'streaking away down the touchline' only to be caught inches short of the line or at the corner flag.

He was well-qualified for the winger's role, being blessed with the genuine speed that made him the county sprint champion for the same year. The Welsh Secondary Schools' selectors were bound to be interested and, sure enough, in 1956 the international cap duly followed. Two items of good news arrived at the same time: he would be playing against England at Gloucester – and he would be on the boat to South Africa. Among the congratulatory messages to be delivered at the family home in the Dunraven Hotel in Cwmgwrach was a letter from a Mr S F Simmons, the manager of the Midland Bank in Glynneath. Unfortunately, his warm and encouraging sentiments did not

The two Young Dragons from Neath Grammar School - Clive Phillips (left) and Rhys Thomas

extend so far as a cash prize from the bank! Clive was not the type of young man to worry about such things; representing his country was honour enough.

In South Africa, he played in three games – against Eastern Transvaal, Western Transvaal and Griqualand West. Suitably, he marked his final appearance at Kimberley with a try.

Even while he was on tour Clive was preparing for his next move. He had already applied for training in dentistry at Guy's Hospital in London and the news that his 'A' Level results had confirmed his entry was the best possible fillip. For the next five years he intended to concentrate on gaining his professional qualifications while also playing a bit of rugby. The latter was, however, cut short. After several games for Guy's in the prestigious and highly competitive Hospitals' Cup competition, a serious knee cartilage injury ended his rugby playing days. The major focus of his time in London, though, was achieved. In July 1961 he left Guy's fully qualified as a dentist and he also married Sylvia, his fiancé from Farnborough. Together they set up home in Islington, from where Clive began his career and Sylvia continued as a nurse. A year later they moved back to South Wales and settled in Porthcawl.

The seaside town was the perfect location for them, with Clive, the former rugby player now proving to be the formidable golfer at the renowned local club, Royal Porthcawl. Meanwhile, after initially working in Swansea, he was also establishing a well-regarded dental practice in Port Talbot. But fate was to deliver a couple of serious blows to Clive. In 1973 he was diagnosed with cancer but courageously overcame the illness. As if to confirm his rediscovered health, two years later he completed a parachute jump and after that pursued all his favourite outdoor activities such as mountain climbing. Tragically, one final illness was still to come. In 1983 he contracted viral hepatitis and died in hospital on 26 January at the age of 45.

Richard Griffiths (Tonypandy Grammar School)
Born: 29 October 1938 5'10" 11st 0lb Centre Tour Number: 18

There was no shortage of attacking talent among the Young Dragons and Richie Griffiths was regarded as one of its brightest exponents. In some ways, he now concedes, the expectations centring on him proved to be something of a burden. These expectations were based not only on his own undoubted ability that had seen him win Wales under-15 caps against England and the South of Scotland in 1954 and become a sprint champion in the Rhondda. They were multiplied by the reputation of one of his elder brothers who had toured South Africa a year earlier and in even more esteemed company. Gareth Griffiths had won the first of his dozen Wales' caps at the age of 21, had been a member of both the Cardiff and Wales' teams that beat New Zealand in 1953, and, crucially, in 1955 had starred for the British Isles in three epic test matches against the Springboks. The otherwise generous hosts never let Richie forget the latter in 1956. Wherever he went as a Young Dragon he was flagged up as 'the brother of the Lion Gareth Griffiths'. It was, of course, a compliment but also, inadvertently, an unwanted attention for the young Richie.

His comparative youth in 1956 is something he still reflects on. He says,

Richie Griffiths (left) and Maurice Palmer on safari at Kruger National Park

'I was too young to get as much out of the tour as I should have done. In some respects I didn't fully appreciate what was going on. Perhaps I simply didn't have the self-confidence to make the most of it.' This fascinating and frank admission is largely at odds with the reflections of many of his team-mates and their own experiences but is nevertheless a very valid observation. What's more, the retrospection is a unique insight into a sensitive individual who in the red jersey and out on the pitch was one of the most dashing young centres of his generation. Though he had only won his first secondary schools cap a couple of months before the tour, he was to go on to win five more in 1957 and 1958 as he completed his schooldays at Tonypandy Grammar School. (Tellingly, the South African publicists even listed Richie's school wrongly – all the programmes show it to be 'Porth County', the alma mater of Gareth).

Ignoring the inevitable comparisons as best he could, Richie still left his mark out on the pitch on his own terms. His debut was against the Eastern Transvaal Country XV at Ermelo and it has to be described as having a 'Boys Own' impact: after 10 minutes he opened the scoring with a try; soon afterwards he broke through and gave a scoring pass to co-centre David Johnston; that was quickly followed by his own second try; in the second half he completed a personal hat-trick. We can see what the South African press were getting at. Eventually Richie played in four of the tour games but admits to being disappointed at missing the centre-piece at Ellis Park.

In September 1958 Richie started a degree course in mathematics and chemistry at Cardiff University and also joined the rugby club at the Arms Park. He is again candid when he says his experiences in first-class rugby were not particularly happy. The Griffiths' brotherhood was again a factor. Gareth was about to take his temporary leave of Cardiff to play for a while for Llanelli, the second oldest brother, John, had already been and gone from the Arms Park and was enjoying his rugby at Treorchy. After 37 first and second team games spread over two seasons in the city, Richie would eventually follow him there and continue playing until his mid-thirties.

Later, Richie's kid brother David would make a name for himself as an outstanding full back for the Bridgend club after a handful of games for Cardiff.

Richie began his teaching career with two years at Gilfach Goch, then had five happy years at Pentre Grammar School, working in the same physics department as Eddie Thomas, a fine forward who had helped Cardiff beat the All Blacks and led them to another famous victory over the Wallabies. In later years Richie also taught at the Upper Rhondda Comprehensive School, was head of mathematics at Cymmer and then Ysgol Gyfun y Cymer, before retiring at the age of 58.

Richie today, enjoying his retirement near Brecon.

For many years he lived in the Rhondda Valley in a house of which he oversaw the building but, ever the pragmatist, eventually looked elsewhere because the lawns there took two days to mow – they were on a hillside! Since 2000 he has lived in Talgarth in a setting he describes as 'delightful'.

John Elgar Williams (Amman Valley Grammar School)

Born: 8 December 1937 5'7" 9st 9lb Utility Back Tour Number: 19

For John Elgar Williams, the trip to South Africa was to be the mere beginning of a long journey to glory, success and long term influence with Welsh Secondary Schools' rugby. No one in 1956 could possibly have predicted how the young utility back from the Amman Valley would go on to hold every important office for both the Secondary Schools and then the reconstituted Welsh Schools' Rugby Union (Senior Group). Yet that's what he did, becoming one of the most important figures in schools rugby in the Principality over a period of three decades. By the 1980s he was following in the footsteps of Ned Gribble, Rowley Jones and all the other teachers with the Young Dragons and managing and coaching national teams himself at home and abroad.

Prior to the South African adventure, John Elgar had only limited opportunities for making his mark in the first choice team. A fine centre or fly-half for his school, his abilities had been recognised with a cap in the match against Yorkshire at Newport in January 1956. He was then a travelling reserve for the games against France and England but there was very little doubt that he would be included in the final tour party of 28. The exhaustive series of district and international trials throughout the season – he reckons there were as many as eleven – gave every aspiring player a chance to display his talents. The official selection listed John Elgar as an utility back but the fates would decree that he would eventually make only one tour appearance and that as a centre.

Before then, there was the usual excitement of pre-tour preparations. In his case they included several presentations, including a watch from his local rugby club at Brynamman, an electric razor from his chapel, and an appearance on the stage during a full school assembly. Now there was no escaping the limelight! He was particularly fascinated by the weekend camp at RAF St Athan. He recalled, 'Cliff Morgan and all the other 1955 Lions had a lot of anecdotes from their time in South Africa but also some solid and sensible advice. One thing that sticks in my mind was that we should remember that we were going to be visitors and guests in a foreign land. We were warned that we would be seeing things like the shanty towns that might horrify us but that we should never criticise aspects of South African life. It was very much a case of When in Rome.... We all came to realise that the Lions had been talking a lot of sense.'

But there was also no shortage of sights and features of the huge new land to be impressed with. 'Like nearly all of the team I hadn't done any travelling of note but some of the things I saw in South Africa made me think about our own lifestyle back home. There was no denying the fact that, for instance, their cars and houses were a level above what we were used to in Wales. And, of course, we were still recovering from the war years and their aftermath and what was particularly noticeable was the quality and quantity of food, especially fresh fruit, available over there.'

On a rugby front, though, John Elgar was to suffer a personal disappointment. Having sat out the first game at Port Elizabeth, he was literally bursting with enthusiasm for his debut in the next match at Bloemfontein. Sadly, his energy was to remain largely untapped. Though he enjoyed a fine game alongside David Johnston – one report noted that they 'were more than a match for the home centres with their devastating tackling' – his playing contribution to the tour was about to end prematurely. It emerged later that a badly sprained ankle was serious enough to sideline him for the remaining six games.

Out of the disappointment and frustration, and probably unknowingly, the seeds of his later eminent career as a coach were sown. With another of the walking wounded, Clive Rowlands, John Elgar was soon made to feel useful. For the next three weeks both of them assisted Rowley Jones and Gwynfor Davies with the training sessions. He remembers, 'It was nothing too elaborate but nevertheless productive for us. They asked me, for instance, to keep an eye on the accuracy and speed of the passing among the backs – and I really valued being involved.'

The injuries to the two West Walians also had their lighter side. John Elgar explains, 'In an effort to ensure that we received expert medical advice, the teachers rearranged the billeting roster so that Clive and I stayed with doctors and their families at our next two stops in Ermelo and Springs. So we found ourselves staying

Centres come in all sizes - John Elgar Williams (left) with Brian Skirrow at Kimberley

with a Dr van der Wathe, which seemed a very sensible situation. Unfortunately he turned out to be a vet! And the other doctor we stayed with was a doctor of philosophy.' The best laid plans…

John Elgar still benefited from his observations of the play of the team and the *modus operandi* of the teachers as the tour moved on to Johannesburg and beyond. 'To watch the skills and team work in the victory over Transvaal was a real pleasure. One moment stands out. We were under pressure behind our own line but instead of the first player hurriedly kicking the ball clear it was passed along the line to the open side and then when there was plenty of time and space it was punted downfield and well away from our territory. In its own way that was a defining moment of the tour, a real testimony to the benefits of everyone playing together and for each other.'

Teamwork was a quality that loomed large in John Elgar's later teaching and coaching career. He reveals, 'What came out of that tour was the importance of camaraderie, of fostering togetherness, and it was something I tried to instil in teams that I took on tour.'

Following his return from South Africa, he immediately entered Swansea University to take a degree in history and after that a year at Loughborough College for his teaching qualification. Then in September 1960 he returned to his *alma mater*, Amman Valley Grammar School, to begin a distinguished 32-year career that culminated in a deputy headship. In the early years he also played first-class rugby, with seven seasons at Llanelli that also included a couple of international trials. His greatest contribution to rugby in Wales still lay ahead. In 1968 he was elected to the committee of the Wales Schools' Rugby Union (Senior Group), eventually becoming its secretary, chairman and coach. It was by any standards an exceptional record of service to the younger generation of sportsmen. But as he says himself, 'The highlight for me is when a former student greets me with "If it hadn't been for you, sir…"'

John Elgar Williams retired from teaching in 1992 and lives in Ammanford.

Brian Alexander Skirrow (Cardiff High School)

Born: 24 December 1938 6′2″ 13st 0lb Wing Tour Number: 20

Brian Skirrow's achievements as a rugby player and administrator are forever linked with South Africa. In 1956 he was a Young Dragon; in 1995 he was working for the International Rugby Board and was Tournament Co-ordinator for the third Rugby World Cup finals. It was quite a responsibility, including as it had already done the organising of the qualifying rounds spread over the previous three years and then the finals themselves with specific tasks spanning from the formulation of the tournament's budgets right across to such practical essentials as flight and transport arrangements. Brian proved equal to all the challenges confronting him, a skill honed by his many years in business and before that the life-changing experience of being a Young Dragon in 1956.

His schoolboy rugby credentials were impeccable. Another gifted centre from Cardiff High School, Meirion Roberts, had captained Welsh Secondary Schools in 1953 before going on to win senior honours and to be part of the Barbarians team that beat the Springboks in 1961. Brian succeeded him in the school team. He was a tall and powerful threequarter, equally at home at centre or on the wing, and went on to captain the first XV for two years. In February 1955 he was in midfield for Cardiff & District Schools against the touring South African High Schools at Cardiff Arms Park. The match was drawn 3-all with Brian making the only try for his wing with what he describes as 'a scoring pass from behind my back' . The *Western Mail* noted, 'Bert [*sic*] Skirrow and Tony Rees were smart Cardiff centres'. In 1956 he won his Welsh Secondary Schools' caps playing on the wing against France and England. He continued in that position on tour in South Africa, appearing against Eastern Transvaal, where he picked up a shoulder injury, and Griqualand West, with his contribution in the latter game earning another approving report from a local newspaper: 'Skirrow played brilliantly on the wing'.

Brian describes the wider experience of South Africa as 'phenomenal'. He continues: 'For me it was all about broadening horizons. There was the travel, of course, all on a scale unimaginable before we left home. The vastness of the country had to be seen to be believed – and it also opened my eyes to some of the simmering social problems out there. But there was also the sheer friendliness of the people and the tremendous hospitality. All in all I found myself on a massive learning curve.' He is also full of praise for the friendships that were forged among the tour party, claiming with just a glimmer of tongue in cheek, that 'I was shy and retiring – unlike Jack Davies'.

With his eighteenth birthday still several months in the future, Brian returned from the tour and went straight back into the sixth form and set for another season as captain. But his final year at school was disrupted on two fronts. Soon after Christmas he picked up a cartilage

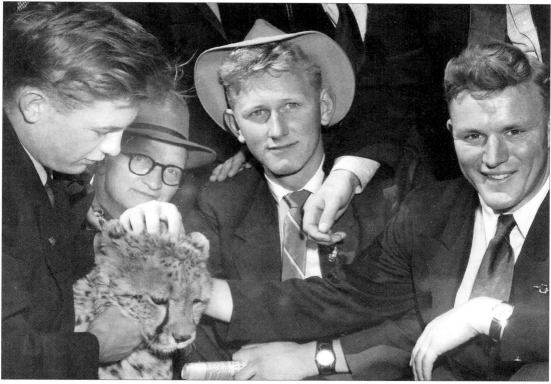

The wildlife held no fears for Brian Skirrow and his friends

injury playing against Monmouth School. His school rugby days were over and he also decided to forego his formal educational qualifications. Instead by June 1957 he took a temporary job with an insurance company before beginning his National Service in the Army the following September. This, too, was to be cut short, as Brian remembers with impressive detail: 'I was in the Royal Signals stationed at Catterick and my army career lasted exactly one year and 55 days.' A perforated ear drum meant a premature demobbing in the autumn of 1958, a return for a while to the world of insurance, before beginning 27 years work in marketing for the Esso Petroleum Company. This was followed by a new role as managing director of Coil Color in Newport before out of the blue in the early 1990s the International Rugby Board advertised for a Tournaments Director for the forthcoming Rugby World Cup.

Urged on by his family, Brian was about to become directly involved again with the world of rugby. His playing days had continued while in the army with a few games for Cardiff and Cardiff Athletic and later with Cathays HSOB in the city but now he was to be at the very heart of the global game. It was a role he thoroughly enjoyed.

Based at the then IRB headquarters in Bristol he worked with the chairman, Keith Rowlands, and from there he literally travelled the world. He says, 'I actually enjoyed the hectic lifestyle with all the travelling and for weeks on end living out of a suitcase. There was one occasion when I left Bristol for Heathrow on a Monday morning, was back on Thursday, but in the meantime had attended an important meeting in Sydney!' At the same time, high profile events were coming along at regular intervals, first cutting his teeth at the IRB World Sevens in Murrayfield in 1993 and then the big one in South Africa two years later. In 1997, after another two years of hard work, Brian decided to retire. Another hectic trip to Hong Kong had been followed by a nasty bout of deep vein thrombosis and what for a time seemed an even more serious incapacity. The time had come to slow down a bit and Brian wisely did just that. The IRB had relocated his offices to Dublin but Brian still lives near Bristol, content with what he has achieved both inside and outside rugby.

Dewi Robinson (Mountain Ash Grammar School)

Born 2 February 1938 5'3" 9st 7lb Fly Half Tour Number: 21

Dewi Robinson was the first-choice fly-half for the majority of the 1955 international season with the selectors accommodating Alan Rees in the centre. For him it had been an auspicious baptism into top-class junior rugby, highlighted by two impressive performances against the touring South African Schools' side. Even though North Glamorgan lost narrowly to the tourists at Merthyr, the *Western Mail* reported that the visitors 'had no one behind the scrum to match the elusiveness of the diminutive fly-half, D Robinson'. His second game against them, for the full Wales XV, was more successful. Reports again referred to him continually instigating attacks from long-range and both wings scored tries in a notable 6-3 victory.

In 1956, however, Dewi had to be content with being a travelling reserve for the three home internationals but with his displays of the previous season still fresh in the memory, allied to consistently fine play for his school and in the trial matches, there was little doubt that he would be an automatic choice for the South African trip. Fellow Mountain Ash old boy Dai Jones describes him as 'a classy fly-half' and his performances on the tour underlined that assessment. His opportunities may have been limited but he steered the backs to convincing attacking rugby in the victories over Western Transvaal and Griqualand West.

Dewi was another player who had little time to bask in the glory of the tour. Three days after his return he, too, began his National Service in the RAF. Having declared his interests as photography and flying he was duly trained as a ground radar fitter. He continued to play rugby for his station teams at RAF Locking and RAF Halton and also for London Welsh before his sporting ambitions were interrupted by a bout of truly active service. While some of his former Young Dragons' team-mates enjoyed regular services' rugby around the British Isles for a couple of years Dewi found himself posted overseas to Cyprus. On the face of it that must have been a rude awakening, coming at a time when the Mediterranean island was locked in the middle of the ugly Turkish/Greek EOKA crisis. The jury remains out on whether the young fly-half was actually called upon to use his military training in anger: many years later the magazine of Cantonian High School where he spent the majority of his teaching career concluded, 'He spent two years lazing about in the sunshine on the beautiful island of Cyprus!'

In 1958 Dewi was demobbed, presumably with an enviable

Dewi Robinson was a keen photographer but on this occasion went in front of the lens at school in 1992.

sun tan, and began a three-year course in handicrafts and general science at Loughborough College. While there he resumed his playing career with games for both the first and second teams. His teaching career commenced in Cardiff in September 1961 at the then Waterhall School. This was eventually reorganised in 1968 into the Cantonian High School and in 33 years' service at both schools he tried his hand at most things. At various times he taught woodwork, metalwork and technical drawing and then careers before becoming a senior year tutor. Dewi's generation of teachers were notable for their ready involvement in extra-curricular activities and in his case they included a photographic club, drama productions and the Duke of Edinburgh Award scheme. Inevitably, he also assisted with games and for eleven years took an adult education evening class. Though teaching in the capital city, Dewi never forgot his rugby roots and Dai Jones swears that whenever he saw him play he invariably wore the black and white socks of Pontypridd RFC. He was also a very enthusiastic golfer.

Dewi took early retirement from teaching in the summer of 1994. The Cantonian magazine, having enviously pondered over his sun-soaked national service, paid due tribute to his work in education. It noted: 'His knowledge and dedication, together with his love and enthusiasm for the craft and technology subjects he taught, had a knock on effect with his colleagues and the pupils he taught over the years. He was forever coming up with new ideas and projects in order to keep abreast of the ever-changing trends in craft and technology . . . The school is losing a very dedicated, conscientious and able teacher and administrator. We wish [his wife] Ann and Dewi a long, happy and active retirement.'

Sadly, this was not to be. Barely nine months after his retirement Dewi died suddenly of a heart attack on 13 April 1995 at the age of 57.

Maurice Sambrook Palmer (Haverfordwest Grammar School)

Born: 7 March 1939 5'9" 11st 4lb Scrum-Half Tour Number: 22

'He was and is the travelling man'. Such is the assessment of Maurice Palmer by one of his 1956 team mates. The allusion to travel, apparently, was to imply that the budding scrum-half was always destined to 'go places' in his professional career as well as in his rugby activities. If so, it is a pretty astute comment on someone who was one of the youngest of Young Dragons on the tour. He would eventually became captain of the Welsh Secondary Schools team in 1958, partner the classical Oxford, England and Lions fly-half Richard Sharp in the Varsity Match, and, when his playing days were over, be so successful in the world of marketing that he founded his own company.

Back in 1956 there was no shortage of schoolboy enthusiasm in everything Maurice did. He had always been prepared to play in any position behind the scrum in order to get a game of rugby. In previous years he had played at fly-half in both a Wales Schools' under-15 final trial match and, after originally being selected at centre, for Pembrokeshire Schools against the touring team from the Eastern Transvaal. In the latter match he was still several weeks short of his sixteenth birthday and almost certainly the youngest player on the pitch. But scrum-half was his preferred position and his enthusiasm paid off. In September 1955 he began the first of his three years as school rugby captain and, further afield, was called up to the seemingly endless sequence of trial matches.

He recalls, 'Every possible combination of teams was put together to unearth the best players to go to South Africa at the end of the school year. So for me that meant playing for Pembrokeshire and Cardiganshire against Carmarthenshire, then the two counties combined against the rest of West Wales, then a wider West Wales XV against West Glamorgan, and so on. You name it, they selected it!'

All the extra games on top of his school matches were worth the sacrifice and effort. Eventually, Maurice worked his

Local alderman James John makes a very formal presentation to Maurice Palmer before the tour.

way through to the final trial of all before the 28 players for the tour were named. On 14 March 1956 at Neath he played in the Black XV against the Reds and soon afterwards was named as one of the three scrum-halves who would become Young Dragons. It was a big moment for him, topped by the further news that he would win his first secondary schools' cap against France at Cardiff Arms Park at the beginning of April.

As with everyone else he had the perfect send-off to the tour. 'All of the county council gave their full support to myself and John Ebsworth, who was the other Pembrokeshire player in the team. The local alderman, James John, whose son Osmonde later became president of the Welsh Rugby Union, presented me with a watch and Haverfordwest Rugby Club gave me a pair of rugby boots.' Clearly the two Pembrokeshire lads were already regarded as ambassadors for the county and this was only the beginning. When Maurice returned in September both he and John Ebsworth were greeted at Haverfordwest and Pembroke Dock railway station stations repectively by the mayor, the town clerk and a bevy of officials from the rugby club. Such was the magic of the Young Dragons.

Maurice learnt many things on the tour. 'On the voyage out I gradually became the fittest I had ever been as a rugby player. We had never had fitness training of such intensity or expertise before and in the weeks ahead it certainly paid off. We also had brine baths, another totally new experience and something I didn't forget in a hurry!' He also reiterates a lesson that other Young Dragons have mentioned – to respect South African society for what it was at the time. What had been first outlined in the pre-tour camp at RAF St Athan was underlined again by the tour manager Claude Mullan, the principal of Springs Boys' High School, when they arrived.

'I won't deny that some of the things I saw struck an odd note. There was I from a traditional socialist and Methodist background encountering apartheid almost at first hand. At one point I was billeted with a Dutch Reform Church minister, a very nice man but one who also had non-whites as his servants. For them it was the natural state of things; for me it was strange. Yet it was also an openly religious society. John Ebs and I invariably had to say prayers before every meal with the families we stayed with and all the people we met were incredibly hospitable. And, of course, physically it is a wonderful country and a privileged experience for us just to be there.'

In playing terms, Maurice's tour was undoubtedly a success. With three scrum-halves in the squad opportunities might have been limited but Clive Rowlands' injury in the second match meant that Maurice and Howard Merrick were always likely to busy. In Maurice's case he went from strength-to-strength. Having made his debut in the third game at Ermelo, he went on to play in another four of the remaining five fixtures. After his first game he wrote home: 'I played [against Eastern Transvaal Country] and I think I had a good game because the masters complimented me afterwards....On Saturday we are playing against Transvaal at Ellis Park so I hope I'll get a game there.'

He needn't have worried. He again partnered Alan Rees at half-back and had what he now regards as his best game of the tour. South African critics agreed. T J Botha, who covered most of the tour, commended him for his 'nippy play', highlighted by two breaks from lineouts, making one try and scoring another. To complete a hectic final week in South Africa, he then played against Griqualand West on the following Monday and Boland 48 hours after that. Including the Transvaal match, he had partnered each of the three fly-halves – Rees, Dewi Robinson and Ieuan Jones – in turn.

Adaptability was a byword with Maurice. He still had two years left in school, completing his 'A' Levels and gaining a place at Oxford. He packed a lot into that period, captaining school, county and country and finishing with half-a-dozen secondary schools' caps.

Maurice was also attracting attention outside Pembrokeshire. As early as January 1955 he had been invited to consider joining the Welch Regiment, the letter written by no less a figure

Maurice, Guto Davies and team mates on tour

than Lieut-Colonel B T V Cowey, himself an international wing of the 1930s. But National Service had finished by the time he left Oxford. At university, the undoubted highlight was his Blue in 1960 but even while studying at Jesus College he found time to play for several other teams, including his home club of Llangwm, the Harlequins (his confirmation letter from them revealing 'It was someone very high up in the Welsh Rugby Union that asked us to get you to play for us and I know he will be pleased that you have agreed'), and Llanelli.

There were also the prestigious invitation teams of the era, Ranji Walker's XV and the Irish Wolfhounds. With a typical glint in his eye he still recalls, 'I played for so many different sides at Stradey Park that I helped to open their new clubhouse three times!'

His life was equally diverse off the field. Having started as a sales development engineer with Foseco Ltd in Tamworth in 1961 he progressed through the Morgan Crucible Group, Bowater and finally became International Marketing Director of Acoustic Research. By 1977 he was ready to set up and become chairman of Maurice Palmer Associates, a highly successful marketing consultancy. He had long since hung up his playing boots, though not before he had added the clubs of Bedford, Lichfield, Saracens and Hoylake and the county sides of Pembrokeshire, Staffordshire and Oxfordshire to his roll of honour.

Now Maurice lives in Little Shelford, an Oxford man happily settled in a Cambridgeshire village … but as was said, he is a travelling man.

Daniel Clive Thomas Rowlands (Ystradgynlais Grammar School)

Born: 14 May 1938 5'10" 11st 12lb Scrum-Half Tour Number: 23

Clive Rowlands has many claims to fame in a long and illustrious career as a scrum-half, coach and administrator: captain of Wales in all 14 of his senior international matches in the 1960s; coach of the all-conquering national team of the 1970s; manager of the British and Irish Lions team that beat the Wallabies in 1989; president of the Welsh Rugby Union in 1989-90. The list of achievements and accolades is endless. Yet perhaps the novelty of his first-ever appearance in a Welsh jersey against Eastern Province in 1956 would cause astonishment among historians of the game: he played at wing-forward. The future controller of Triple Crown and Five Nations championship winning teams from the base of the scrum cut his teeth as a junior international as part of a Welsh pack.

The circumstances surrounding Clive's debut that afternoon in Port Elizabeth were entirely unplanned. He explains, 'I was not expecting to play in that game at all. Howard Merrick had been named as scrum-half in the team and as there were no replacements in those days I was expecting to spend the afternoon watching the game from the grandstand. But in the coach on the way to the ground our open-side wing-forward Leighton Davies was suffering from flu symptoms. So it was decided that as a precaution Leighton shouldn't play and that I was the new (in every sense of the word) wing-forward. I always knew my first game for Wales would be something memorable but I hadn't expected this!' Typically, Clive, playing in borrowed boots, rose to the occasion, giving 100 per cent effort though the pack, with Jack Davies injured, were eventually outgunned as the Young Dragons were beaten for the first and only time on the tour. But the rookie wing-forward had acquitted himself well. He was reported to have been 'alive and alert' (!) and had the satisfaction of scoring his team's second try in the closing stages.

Four days later he was on more familiar territory when selected as scrum-half for the game against Orange Free State. It was an occasion he was relishing. 'Obviously I would feel more comfortable in my normal position but there was the added bonus of having Alan Rees as my half-back partner. He was a beautiful player, easily the most naturally talented back in the party, a lovely kicker of the ball and blessed with a beautiful pair of hands.'

All, then, was set for a memorable match but for Clive it was to end disastrously. Midway though the second half he fell to the rock hard ground after a tackle and broke his collarbone. In playing terms at least, his tour was over. He admits to a feeling of frustration and despair but as one of the uncapped players in the squad he had the satisfaction of representing his country for the first time. There was a happy post-script when a year later the officers of the Welsh Secondary Schools belatedly awarded him a cap. And out of the deep disappointment of the premature end to his playing days as a Young Dragon there was born the first tentative steps of an unforgettable coaching career. Along with his great friend John Elgar Williams he was drafted in as an observer and assistant to Rowley Jones and Gwynfor Davies at team training sessions. 'I enjoyed that because I was being made to feel part of something useful – and I certainly learnt a lot.'

What Clive missed out on in a playing sense he made up for in the social side of the tour. 'What made everything easier from the very start was that most of us were great friends before we left Southampton. One thing about all those trial matches in Wales throughout the previous winter – and, of course, the seasons prior to that – was that we were forever catching buses together to travel across South Wales and we all got to know each other. So the tour was in some ways a natural continuation of what we had been experiencing at home – but with a bit more luxury!'

Several other Young Dragons testify to the mischievous young Rowlands charming his way into the good books of his hosts at various stopovers and, certainly, there was no shortage of gifts

Clive Rowlands in his first Welsh jersey (and Leighton Davies' boots) at Port Elizabeth.

Friends for life - John Elgar Williams and Clive on the *Arundel Castle*

showered on him and whoever was fortunate (usually John Elgar Williams) to be billeted with him. It also helped that Clive, whilst having private concerns about the huge differences in living standards he saw between the races, liked South Africa a lot. He explains, 'South Africa is more like Wales than we sometimes appreciate. Leaving aside the sheer size of the country and of course the weather, there are several similarities – we both have two languages, there is a common love of cricket and rugby, and we are great singers!'

He exempts David Walkey from the latter – 'Hopeless singer but David was a very good captain, a remarkable public speaker and a fine all-round athlete.' In the end, Clive enjoyed the tour. His arrival home was saluted by the neighbourhood with the traditional presentations and then it was into the RAF. After his initial induction he was eventually stationed at Yatesbury in Wiltshire, St Mawgan in Cornwall and then Innsworth and trained as an air radar mechanic. His collarbone injury from South Africa curtailed his rugby for the best part of another year, not helped by further injuries, but he remained active playing soccer and again did some coaching. In September 1958 Clive began a three-year course at Cardiff Training College where he again rubbed shoulders with someone who would influence his later coaching, Roy Bish. 'I was fortunate to be there at that time because Roy was one of the great pioneers of coaching in Wales. I was impressed by his methods and it was no surprise when he went on to coach a very successful Cardiff club side.'

Clive also had his eyes on first-class rugby and he jumped at the chance to play for Llanelli, periodically, for a couple of seasons. He also considers it a great honour to have been chosen as college captain for two years but soon he was making his mark further afield. Combining his embryonic teaching career at Coed Eva School in Monmouthshire with club rugby at Pontypool, he quickly found himself in the captain's role again. In what was to be a momentous season for him in 1962-63, he became captain of club and country. Other players have captained Wales on their international debut but none have gone on to retain that responsibility for any length of time. Clive, however, did so for three full seasons, an overseas tour (appropriately to South Africa in 1964), and 14 caps that culminated in Wales' first Triple Crown for 13 years. He finished his playing career in 1967-8 with the captaincy of Swansea and immediately after that became national coach.

The rest, as they say, is history. Under his guidance the great stars of the 1970s developed and delivered further glories to a hungry Welsh public. The attributes of Clive, the ultimate Welshman, were recognised in the wider rugby fraternity as he became manager of the erstwhile British Isles touring team that was due to visit South Africa in 1986. When that was called off he managed the team in the International Rugby Board's centenary matches of the same year and, three years later, headed the next Lions' squad that went to Australia. On his return to Wales he became WRU president in 1989-90, thus emulating the achievement of one of his teachers in 1956, T Rowley Jones. He is also president of the Welsh Schools' Rugby Union. For Clive Rowlands, the wheel has come full circle.

Being a Young Dragon had set Clive off on an incredible journey. Today, he still lives in Upper Cwmtwrch and counts the 1956 adventure as something he will always treasure.

Neville John Johnson (Bassaleg Grammar School)

Born: 9 August 1938 5'11" 15st 0lb Prop Tour Number: 24

No one was in any doubt that Nev Johnson was a prop forward. If nothing else his thick-set frame meant that he *looked* like one – but he was very much an anchor of the pack on the field as well, an assessment borne out by his playing career before, during and after the tour. In 1953 he represented Wales under-15s against England when Howell Morgan was his fellow prop and David Walkey packed down behind him in the second row; he won secondary schools' caps against France as both a prop (in Toulon in 1955) and a second row (at Cardiff Arms Park in 1956); and in later years had a fearsome reputation in senior rugby as a member of an outstanding Newport pack.

Originally a pupil at New Tredegar Technical Institute, his later school years were spent at Bassaleg Grammar School where Walkey was the captain. They were also the Monmouthshire props when the county played the South African High Schools at Abertillery in 1955. On tour as a Young Dragon he was particularly busy, appearing in the first three games and six in all.

Nev admits to having 'fabulous memories' of his time in South Africa. He says, 'On the voyage out, the amazing food on offer was an obvious attraction but I was reminded in no uncertain terms that we eat to live, not live to eat! As we eventually approached landfall at Cape Town there were the incredible Cape Rollers and, yes, you could literally smell the scent of Africa as it awaited us.' Not surprisingly, Nev was the sort of young man who got on well with everyone he came into contact with. Thus, 'My first introduction to the Bantus was being greeted while still on board as they were unloading the ship and this little guy looked at my blazer badge and said "You beat those Springbok bastards, massa!" These days they tell me they support the Springboks but when Dave Walkey scorched over for a try in the corner at Ellis Park the umbrellas and top hats went up in the air at the segregated end behind the posts – and continued to do so every time we scored.'

Clearly, Nev's tour was as eventful as anybody's with even the offer of a rather unusual job. 'I was offered a job at the Skyline Hotel playing the drums after sitting in with a very doubtful band leader. Truly, they offered me £20 a week, plus board and lodging and, wait for it, a *bar allowance!* Now just consider this: when I started teaching five years later I was earning less than a tenner a week. I often wonder what

Perfecting front row techniques. Nev Johnson, Dai Jones and David Walkey with Gwynfor Davies in training at the Olympic Ground in Port Elizabeth.

would have happened to my rugby career if I had accepted that job.' As we will see, Nev's career path didn't exactly follow a traditional pattern even after he took up teaching back in Wales.

Meanwhile, though, life as a Young Dragon continued to be an eye-opening experience. He says, 'Everything was on a massive scale – the huge barbecues, the Big Hole at Kimberley, and the unexpected panorama of Kruger National Park. Something else I recall is visiting an Afrikaans' church and seeing the stove pipe hats and stern expressions on the elders' faces. In every respect it was an incredible experience for ordinary lads from the valleys of Wales.'

Nev was another individual who swapped the delights of the Dragons for the new life of National Service immediately on his return home. While in the RAF he played for Bomber Command and the full service's side, and further widened his rugby experience with games for Peterborough and London Welsh. Next up was teaching training at St Luke's College where he played for the first XV for two years and also for Devon in the county championship. College vacations provided opportunities to play for Pontypridd before he was invited to join Newport and pack down as loose-head prop to the Lions' test hooker, Bryn Meredith. Life was not all rugby, though, as he adds in typical fashion, 'While at college I married Avis – no shotgun, honest!' His final year of higher education was spent at Cardiff Training College qualifying for his Dip Phys Ed and playing in the same team as Clive Rowlands and Leighton Davies. But it was with the Newport club that he really made a name for himself. He had already been selected for a final international trial in December 1960 before, a month later, he played his part in the first of two epic Black & Amber performances against the giants of world rugby. The record books show that on 11 January 1961 Newport lost 3-nil to the Fifth Springboks; the final score doesn't begin to tell the full story. The touring team were eventually beaten only once in 34 fixtures in Europe, and were still invincible when they reached Newport in the final month of their tour, but the club came closer than any other side at that stage to beating them. Their heroes were the pack in which J B G Thomas reported in the *Western Mail*, 'the front row of Greenslade, Meredith and Johnson stood up extremely well to the Springbok trio and gave them what amounted to a hiding in the struggle for possession.' Sadly, Nev was the only one of the club's eight forwards that day never to win a senior Wales' cap (though he did in later life captain his country at clay pigeon shooting). In 1963 he again earned the plaudits of the critics when Newport went one better, beating the All Blacks at Rodney Parade. His playing career ended prematurely, however, at the age

A prop's appetite. Nev (far right) and friends enjoy another substantial South African meal.

of 27 because of back problems. His connections with the game, though, were far from over. He returned to the club to become coach and then team manager before eventually standing down because of his business commitments.

Nev's career away from rugby has, to say the least, been colourful. After an initial year teaching at Ystrad Mynach College, he taught for the next decade at his village school in Bedwas and for the second half of that time he also became a publican. The latter became a full-time commitment when he and Avis eventually took over the Maenllwyd Inn in Rudry, making it into one of the most popular eating and drinking pubs in the area. That was followed by another change of direction, a building company with one of his sons and, finally, a move to permanent residence in Spain where he and Avis still live. Sport, though, has crept back into his life periodically. He accepted the challenge of coaching a Spanish rugby club, Villa Jiosa, but after three months conceded that 'they had lots of pace and ball skills but no real understanding of the nature of the game'. An assessment, the second part of which, could never be applied to Nev.

Howell John Morgan (Llanelli Grammar School)
Born: 17 May 1938 5'10" 13st 4lb Prop Tour Number: 25

'I was named after Archbishop Howell of Wales' is one of Howell Morgan's proud boasts, firmly with tongue in cheek. It would probably be more appropriate if he had been named after Victor Ludorum or some other standard-bearer of sporting excellence because in his formative years young Howell was himself a sportsman of rare all-round abilities. His athletics' achievements encompassed him being crowned national champion at shot and discus and county champion (as well as captain) for the long jump and 220 yards and he was also a keen gymnast. Not surprisingly, he twice won the Bryn Isaac Memorial Trophy for Junior Sportsman of the Year in his home town. As befitted a pupil of the two notable rugby nurseries of Stebonheath Secondary Modern School and Llanelli Grammar School he was also a junior player of some distinction. He won his under-15 caps for Wales in 1953, playing against England home and away and against Scotland. In 1955 he played for West Wales against the South African High Schools but had to wait until after the Young Dragons' tour before gaining his secondary schools' cap against Yorkshire in 1957. In South Africa he played against Griqualand West at Kimberley.

Off the field, Howell found the tour to be a 'wonderful experience'. He was not alone in highlighting the sight of Table Mountain, the variety of wildlife at the Kruger National Park, and also the challenge of playing on such hard grounds. He was also a proficient goalkicker and admits to being slightly

Howell Morgan with his Wales under-15 cap in 1953.

frustrated at not having an opportunity to demonstrate his skill in a match situation. However, he made up for that by passing on some tips to his hosts. He says, 'I used to take the lads of the families we stayed with, along with their friends, for kick abouts in the evenings on their local fields. Because of the altitude I was surprised how far the ball would travel – but I certainly impressed my young friends when I placed the ball from the halfway line and it flew over the top of the posts and over the dead ball line! It was a shame I did not have the chance to do it in a match.' He is too modest to point out that the following January he saved a losing situation for Wales against Yorkshire by expertly kicking the penalty goal that drew the game at 3-all.

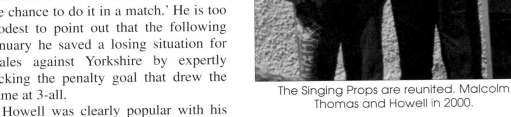

The Singing Props are reunited. Malcolm Thomas and Howell in 2000.

Howell was clearly popular with his hosts in South Africa, admitting that 'they took us into their homes and into their hearts'. He was also an enthusiastic chorister and happily remembers forming a breakaway duo with Malcolm Thomas, 'The Singing Props'. By all accounts they were a great success, augmenting their larger choir's contributions with a few popular songs of their own at after-match functions and dances.

After the tour Howell had another year at school but a bad knee injury forced him to miss the second half of the season after the Yorkshire match. Later in 1957 he began his National Service with the RAF, playing for his camp team as well as Bomber Command and the RAF in representative matches. His all round sporting prowess was still very evident, adding basketball and boxing ('I discovered I was fit but not for boxing') to his athletics and thoroughly enjoying himself. His intention after being demobbed was to go to St Luke's College, Exeter the following autumn and to fill in the months until then with a temporary job and rugby for local clubs in West Wales. Everything went according to plan until the summer immediately before he was due to become a student again. He explains, 'My little body was ruined in a very serious motor cycle accident and I was unable to take up my place at St Luke's. It took six years to stick me together again but I still managed to lose a bit.'

In 1966 Howell retrained as a toolmaker but within four years the strain of his long-standing injuries forced him to find less physical employment. The disappointments were still not quite over. 'By 1980 I was forced to give up work altogether as I was considered unemployable due to my injuries and serious wear and tear to my spine, hips, arm and other parts.'

Since then he has kept active with his hobbies and cycling, refusing to be downhearted by life's setbacks and the need for hospital treatment. Perhaps the singing prop would have made a good archbishop after all.

John Edward Davies (Cowbridge Grammar School)

Born: 5 September 1937 6'1" 12st 11lb Second Row Tour Number: 26

'From first to last the tour was a positive experience. There were absolutely no negatives involved.' John Davies' assessment of his Young Dragons' experience will strike a familiar chord with every one involved with the great adventure of 1956. It also reveals a lot about John, or Jack as he was and still is known by his friends. He would have more reason than most to look back at the trip to South Africa with some disappointment. After all, he was another of the team to be sidelined from action after only one game on tour. In his case it was a truly painful experience. Playing in the opening fixture against Eastern Province, he dislocated his right ankle four minutes before half-time and was forced to leave the field. Not realising the full extent of the injury he returned to the action early into the second half but again limped off 15 minutes before the end of the match. The photograph of his second departure tells its own story with the newspaper caption writer accurately describing his face 'twisted with pain'.

Typically, Jack refused to be downhearted and for a while was impressively optimistic about an early return to fitness. He told the local paper, 'I was going one way, the other fellow was going the other, and there were two chaps on top of me, so what could I do? I'll be back not for the next match but the one after.' Unfortunately for the player and the team the prognosis proved inaccurate and Jack was forced to become the first of the walking (or in his case limping) wounded, soon to be joined at the end of the same week by John Elgar Williams and Clive Rowlands. He admits, 'I was obviously disappointed because I was hopeful that the injury only involved damage to a small bone but the x-ray confirmed

Jack Davies takes the field for what turned out to be his only appearance of the tour at Port Elizabeth.

something far more serious. I had no choice but to accept the situation for what it was and try to be as useful to the team and the tour as I could.'

There was little danger of Jack becoming a peripheral figure. He soon threw all his energies into his role as perennial duty boy, a responsibility he performed with typical thoroughness and energy. One big regret, though, was that he didn't have the opportunity to put into practice the advice he had been given before he left home. Recalling the pre-tour camp at RAF St Athan, he says, 'All of us will have particular memories of that weekend when several of the 1955 Lions' came to talk to us. For me, the stand-out moment was something that Russell Robins said. There had been a lot of advice about having 180-degree awareness when playing but Russell also emphasised the importance of picturing the field of play in your head. The best time to do that was the night before the game, lying in bed and imagining the ceiling as the pitch. Then I should envisage what I might do in specific field positions and play the game in my mind's eye. It was a very interesting idea – but I only had the chance to use it once.'

There was, however, a happy postscript to Jack's bad luck at Port Elizabeth. Eleven years later he returned to the city on another rugby tour. Again it was a 'first'. The Young Dragons had been the first representative team from Wales to tour South Africa; in 1967 Cardiff became the first club side to receive an official invitation to tour the country. Jack, now an experienced 29-year-old lock, was a member of a star-studded team that played five matches. The undoubted highlight was the 34-9 trouncing of Eastern Province at Port Elizabeth. For him, the dark day of 1956 had at last been replaced with the happiest of memories.

A lot of rugby water had passed under the bridge between the two tours. In September 1956 Jack returned to Cowbridge Grammar School for a final year, enthused by the tour and its lessons. He says, 'Before we went the rugby coaching I had received had been fairly rudimentary. On the ship going out it quickly became apparent that Gwynfor Davies and Rowley Jones were preparing us far more thoroughly and expertly for the games ahead. I remembered that in the years that followed and when coaching youth teams tried to follow their example, particularly their management of young players that didn't rely on shouting and bawling.'

Jack (fourth from right) and the team are not too tired to sing at Port Elizabeth station after their 39-hour rail journey from Cape Town.

Jack was also well prepared for his school life in another sense. 'When all the gifts and presentations were made ahead of the tour I was fortunate to receive generous help from the clubs at Llantwit Major and Glamorgan Wanderers. The 1950 Lion Rees Stephens also made a presentation. With the money I received I bought a pair of boots and a tracksuit but my mother insisted that I keep some back to buy a satchel. She said that I was only on the tour for eight weeks but that I had another year of school work!' Fortunately, Jack still played rugby in that year. In the spring of 1957 two more caps were added to the two he had gained a year earlier. The ultimate honour was the captaincy of Wales against England at Cardiff Arms Park. Eight other Young Dragons were in the team, including Graham Davies alongside him in the second row. The match was won 6-5, bringing down the curtain on Jack's schools' rugby career in the best possible fashion.

There followed three happy years studying history at Aberystwyth University, during which time he also played occasionally for Llanelli under the captaincy of the legendary R H Williams, and then a year at Cardiff University to gain his diploma of education. The latter was combined with a season turning out for Pontypridd Rugby Club which, he says, was a good club to join because 'they played good rugby and I made many life long friends.' In 1962 Jack began teaching at Beckenham Grammar School and that meant another change of clubs, this time to London Welsh for two seasons. He returned to Wales in 1964 to teach first at Penarth Grammar School and, after that, Whitchurch Grammar School for nearly thirty years apart from a four-year spell at Ogmore. So began another significant development in Jack's career as a rugby player, coach and administrator. Between 1964 and 1976 he played over 160 games for Cardiff and Cardiff Athletic, the last at the tender age of 39. By then he was on the committee of the Arms Park club, a natural progression for someone who had also captained the Athletic XV for three seasons. In due course he became first team coach and then chairman and had also begun his considerable work for youth rugby in Cardiff and Wales. It was something that gave him tremendous satisfaction. 'When captaining Cardiff Athletic I had always encouraged young players to join the club to play for us as a stepping stone to the first team. But being involved with the youth team gave me even more influence with a greater number of players. We recruited them not just from the city, but the docks, the valleys, anywhere that might have youngsters who wanted regular rugby and where they might feel valued. Even the little things, like establishing the principle of being awarded a Cardiff Youth tie, contributed to this sense of belonging.'

Eventually, Jack extended his service to the Wales Youth set-up and everyone benefited. His honorary work to other organisations in Welsh rugby has also been considerable. As well as being a former secretary of the Cardiff Former Players' Association, he has served on the committee of the Crawshay's club and is still doing sterling work as secretary of the Welsh Academicals. But memories of 1956 are never far away. He says, 'To give two examples from when I returned to South Africa with Cardiff in 1967. Our first game was against South West Africa in Windhoek. In the opposition team was a prop called Jacques Kotze. I hadn't realised the significance of this until he came up to me and said he had played for Boland against the Young Dragons. Then his classic remark was, "I remember your tough prop, Johnson!" Nev would have been pleased with that. Then a couple of weeks later I was looking around the rugby museum at Ellis Park when I spotted our team photograph from 1956. It was great to think that our tour had not been forgotten'

There was little danger of that. With countless years of service to education and youth and senior rugby in Wales John Davies is now retired and lives in Miskin.

Malcolm Wilmot Pemberton (Newport High School)

Born: 15 March 1937 6'2" 13st 0lb Lock Tour Number: 27

Malcolm Pemberton was one of the most gifted all-round sportsmen in the Young Dragons' team. At Newport High School he was captain of rugby, cricket and athletics. In the latter, he was particularly adept in a variety of field events, including high jump, triple jump, long jump plus, most notably, the shot and discus. His father had been an international bowls player, but his elder brother, John, had tragically died during World War Two when the ship on which he was being evacuated to Canada was torpedoed in mid-Atlantic. In later years Malcolm, his wife Cheri, and two sons Guy and Mark were to live and work in Ontario – and, indeed, become Canadian citizens and hold dual nationality.

Malcolm's leadership qualities had also been recognised by the Monmouthshire county selectors when he was appointed as captain for their game against the touring South African Schools at Abertillery Park in 1955. This was a considerable honour because as well as four other future

The all-rounder. Malcolm Pemberton in athletics' action for Oxford University.

Young Dragons – Nev Johnson, John Puddle, Graham Davies and David Walkey – the county pack included a future Wales' captain and British Lion, Alun Pask. The game ended in a 6-all draw with Malcolm rescuing his side with a acrobatic try from the tail end of a lineout as the final whistle beckoned. International honours followed in 1956 when he was capped against England at Gloucester, packing down in the back row with Allan Williams and Leighton Davies. It was a unit that was to serve the Young Dragons well in the early games in South Africa. In their first game together at Bloemfontein it was reported that 'breakaways Williams, Pemberton and Davies were too quick for the Free State backs'. Malcolm went on to play in five games on tour.

On his return home, Malcolm went to Birmingham University and in 1959 completed his BSc degree in Chemistry; from there he transferred to Keble College, Oxford, and eventually gained a doctorate in organic chemistry three years later. Somehow, he still managed to find time for his sporting activities. As well as playing for the first teams at Birmingham University, Keble College and Oxford University, where he narrowly missed selection for a Blue at Twickenham due to injury, he also enjoyed some first-class club rugby in Wales. His debut in the Newport back row in 1956-57 made him one of the youngest forwards to play for the club at that time and he was also selected for Crawshay's XV in special invitation matches. Meanwhile, he was also winning senior international honours in athletics, most notably in the 1958 when he represented Wales in the British Empire & Commonwealth Games and finished eighth in the discus. In 1961 he gained an athletics Blue at Oxford, competing against Cambridge at the White City Stadium and also for the combined universities against Harvard & Yale, a high profile event of the period.

A flourishing career and a varied involvement in sport continued to go hand in hand in the 1960s. With his DPhil qualification under his belt Malcolm worked as a technical officer in research and development with ICI Plastics Division between 1962 and 1967. This based him at Welwyn Garden City and, naturally, he joined the local rugby club He was still only 26 but his first experience there was, to say the least, noteworthy. Having turned up one Saturday afternoon looking for a game he was asked in what position he played. In response to back row he was told, 'Well, today you're on the wing for the fifths'. Malcolm duly scored three tries. A year later he was appointed first team captain and in 1965 he also played county rugby for Hertfordshire. In his second season in charge in 1965-66 he led Welwyn to their most successful season – 24 wins and two draws in 27 fixtures, with the only defeat against high-flying London Welsh. In later years he also coached the club, occasionally played in the lower sides to encourage the youngsters, and in 1971-72 was invited to captain the first team for a third time.

From 1967 to 1989 Malcolm worked for the Diversey Corporation, an international speciality chemical company, first as its Manufacturing and Technical Director for the UK and Europe and then, from 1981, as its Senior Vice President based in Toronto. The family relocated to Canada for six years, living in Oakville, Ontario, and soaking up their new environment and culture. Cheri Pemberton assures us that Malcolm maintained his sporting interests, not rugby, perhaps, and certainly not American Football ('right shape ball but everything else about the game was totally alien') but ice hockey and baseball as a spectator and a fatherly interest in his sons playing in the junior soccer leagues.

Following his return to Britain in 1987, Malcolm worked for two more years as the Director of Europe and Chairman Diversey Technology from the company's Watford office before leaving to become an independent

Malcolm at his desk during his successful career in international chemicals.

industry consultant for a couple of years. In 1991 he was diagnosed with motor neurone disease but, as Cheri says, 'He remained positive and continued to lead as normal a life as possible.' In his final year he was seriously disabled and confined to a wheelchair but continued to support Welwyn RFC from the touchline and in the bar and took a holiday with friends in Venice where with their support he achieved the considerable feat of being lowered into a gondola.

Malcolm died on 1 August 1993, aged 56, five days after he and Cheri, again in the company of a large group of friends, had celebrated their twenty-fifth wedding anniversary.

Alwyn Morris (Neath Technical School)

Born: 11 March 1939 5'11" 12st 0lb Hooker Tour Number: 28

Alwyn Morris was the baby of the party, younger than Maurice Palmer by four days and Dewi Jones by ten; that probably made him a Dragon cub. Whatever, he was another who enjoyed himself, learned a lot, and went on to give great service to the Welsh Secondary Schools' team for another two international seasons. His selection to tour South Africa attracted the customary congratulations and presentations in Aberdulais, where his family lived at the time, though not without one potentially controversial aspect. He explains, 'The local pub was The Dulais Rock and they made a collection from the regulars and it amounted to quite a sum of money. But the local councillor got wind of it and he ruled that if I accepted any cash I would be breaching my amateur status and quickly barred from playing rugby union. So instead there was a token presentation of a nice watch and the rest of the money went to charity.' Ironically, five years later Alwyn voluntarily 'professionalised' himself when he accepted an offer to play rugby league for Doncaster. In the summer of 1956, however, he was very much a star-struck amateur as he set off with the rest of the Young Dragons from Southampton.

He says, 'We were all in what amounted to the lap of luxury, with food coming from all directions, even free ice-cream at any time we wanted it, the daily training sessions that made me fitter than at any time up to then, and the friendships that were a

Alwyn Morris with the son of the Sanders' family, his first hosts in Port Elizabeth

feature of the squad. One thing I didn't like, though, was the albatross that seemed to be following the ship. I kept a wary eye on it and couldn't help wondering whether it was a sign of some doom awaiting us in South Africa!' He needn't have worried. Though playing opportunities proved to be limited, young Alwyn soaked up everything about the strange new land, particularly enjoying his billeting in private homes where he met local people who were good listeners as well as talkers 'though all they wanted to talk to me about a lot of the time was Cliff Morgan and the Lions.'

Alwyn returned to school for more two more years during which he played five internationals for the Secondary Schools, three at prop and his final two in 1958 as a hooker. He also played in the demanding West Wales League for Seven Sisters, which he still regards as a vital part of his rugby education. 'What a great learning zone that was. "Seven" at that time were in the middle of a great era and there were some class players in the team. I thoroughly enjoyed my time with them and am indebted to them for the love and enthusiasm for the game which I have never lost.'

'After I completed my schooling I did a stint on the buses before I took up a place at St Luke's College where I enjoyed some of the most satisfying rugby times of my life. It was a perfect situation – a lovely part of the world, the college itself had attractive buildings and great facilities, everything was PE orientated and we also had the beautiful seaside town of Dawlish nearby. Oh, and I also did some studying.' He played two seasons for the college first XV, where he was re-united with other Young Dragons such as Leighton Davies, Nev Johnson, Dewi Jones and Rhys Thomas as well as future senior internationals Brian Price, Danny Harris and Grahame Hodgson. He adds, 'It was a really exciting team to be involved with and as well as gaining my college colours I played county rugby for Devon and some vacation rugby with Llanelli.'

As he was completing his teacher training Alwyn took the unusual step of 'going north' in every sense, playing rugby league for Doncaster and teaching P E and geography at Wheatley Hills Boys High School in the town. At the same time he began his long involvement in coaching at school, district and county levels. He says, 'It was particularly interesting in that area because in the first couple of years of secondary education the boys played rugby league and then in the next two or three they played union. It worked quite well, too.'

Alwyn taught in Doncaster for nine years before moving to Worcester at the end of 1970. He remained there as Head of P E at Bishop Perowne C E High School for the remainder of his full-time career and is still there in a supply teacher capacity. The latter is all part of a master monetary plan. 'We have a daughter who lives in New Zealand and married to a Maori, which raises interesting rugby possibilities for their son. The "dosh" from the supply teaching goes into the little black box with the silver fern and when it is heavy enough Averil and I set sail for New Zealand for a couple of months.'

The Six Wise Men

Whatever the doubts and uncertainties and many debates within the executive committee of the Welsh Secondary Schools' Rugby Union about the viability of the tour, the six teachers eventually chosen to travel with the players proved to be an ideal management team. Meetings before the Young Dragons left Wales decided that there should be a sharing of responsibilities among the six, but in practice there was a natural evolution of specific roles and profiles.

As chairman, **Edwin Rhys Gribble** was always likely to be regarded as

The six wise men take to the sea. Guto Davies is at the back, Gwynfor Davies at the front with (from left to right) Percy Williams, Ned Gribble, Rowley Jones and Monty Warrington

the tour manager and so it proved. Newspaper reports at home and abroad referred to him as such – he admitted later he became 'resigned' to the perceived role and gave up trying to correct the imposed title – and he was certainly the chief spokesman at impromptu post-match press conferences. At the many social and civic functions he tended to share the duties with the very articulate and able captain, David Walkey. An added attraction for the South African media, inevitably, was that Ned Gribble had coached Cliff Morgan at Tonyrefail Grammar School and, over the years, the fly-half had been generous in his praise of the guidance he had received in his schooldays. It is equally the case that the master was very comfortable to be spoken of in the same breath as the magical Morgan, and no one could blame him for that.

Among the Young Dragons, Ned was regarded as an 'enlightened disciplinarian', an upholder of the traditional virtues, particularly good manners, and his charges were more than happy to comply with his standards. He also never flinched from giving forthright views on South African rugby. At the end of the tour, while commending the organisation that underpinned all their game and the renowned power of their forwards, he added, 'The three-quarter play of your boys seems to lack guile. I have not seen one boy attempt a side-step, or even resort to a variation of pace to create an opening for himself.'

Ned Gribble taught woodwork at Tonyrefail from 1933 until his death in 1961, and in his last years was treasurer of the WSSRU. In April 1962 a memorial service and Welsh Secondary Schools Past v Present match was held at the school. Seven British Lions were included in the Past XV under the captaincy of Cliff Morgan.

Percy Williams was the oldest member of the management team and, indeed, had been a founder member of the schools' union before serving on the executive committee in the 1930s; he had been chairman in 1947-49 and later became president. Remembered as a rather staid, reflective pipe-smoker, Percy was regarded as a quiet tourist who preferred to give his advice discreetly and without too much ceremony. David Walkey pays tribute to him as 'a quiet gentleman, rather soft-spoken and shy and retiring'. On tour he assumed

Percy Williams and Rowley Jones seeing the sights in Port Elizabeth

responsibility for the injured players, ensuring that they received the necessary hospital treatment. Percy taught history at Abertillery Grammar School for most of his career. He died in 1997.

Another senior member of the group was **H S 'Monty' Warrington**, the physical education organiser for Merthyr Tydfil. Originally from Yorkshire and a bachelor, he took on the onerous responsibility of being the 'pocket-money man'. He had also served the executive as its secretary since 1948 and at the age of 60 he regarded the tour as his last farewell before retirement. In fact he carried on until 1960 and he stayed true to his intent of watching schools rather than senior teams 'because they play better rugby'. Also as planned he spent his last years in Penarth, remaining in contact with at least one of the Young Dragons, Graham Davies. In fact, when he died his will bequeathed one of the match balls from South Africa to Graham.

G J 'Guto' Davies was a senior master at Bridgend Grammar School but was originally from Cwmllynfell, where he had family links with Clive Rowlands. Another long-serving member of the executive, he was a past chairman and after the tour became its treasurer for three years. His calm disposition made him another important member of the group in South Africa and he was particularly successful in studying the tactics and methods of the opposition and advising on the team's counter-measures. His namesake, **Gwynfor Davies**, PE master at Queen Elizabeth Grammar School in Carmarthen, was the youngest teacher at the age of 34. Originally from the Garw Valley, he had visited South Africa previously but under very different circumstances. In 1942 he had completed his RAF training as an air bombardier at No 42 Air School in Port Elizabeth; towards the end of the war he had baled out at 18,000 feet from a Lancaster over Germany, qualifying him for membership of the Caterpillar Club. With the altogether more pleasant experience of touring with the Young Dragons he became the coach and fitness expert. In 2006 he was the last surviving member of the management team.

T Rowley Jones retains a special place in the life and times of the Young Dragons. There seems little doubt that without his foresight – and as his son David concedes, his sheer 'bloody mindedness' – the tour would never have happened. John Elgar Williams, himself a leading figure in schools' rugby administration and coaching in later years, makes an interesting observation when he says, 'At the time no one fully appreciated the extent of

Gwynfor Davies and Rowley Jones with some of their South African counterparts.

Rowley's work load. Apart from anything else, he had no precedent to work from, merely his own vision and organising skills.' He also benefited, undoubtedly, from the dedication of his wife, Mary, as together they toiled throughout the long winter of 1955-56 overseeing and driving the fund raising that made the tour a reality.

In 1956 Rowley was a PE teacher at Brynmawr Grammar School; he later became its deputy head. His background was particularly unusual, having received his college training in Denmark where he honed his gymnastic skills. While in the RAF during the war, unusually, he played badminton for Scotland and rugby league for Batley when the divide between rugby union and rugby league was lax. He played rugby union for London Welsh, Pontypool and Ebbw Vale and tennis for Monmouthshire. Throughout his life he was also a keen golfer, with county honours for Monmouthshire. After the tour he became honorary secretary of the WSSRU for 15 years, then fulfilled a similar role for the new Welsh Schools' Rugby Union, and in 1977-78 was a notably successful president of the Welsh Rugby Union, a grand slam season that culminated in a nine-match tour of Australia. But it was secondary schools' rugby that remained closest to his heart and which he counted as his greatest achievement. Rowley retired from teaching in 1979 and in his latter years lived with Mary near their family in Hertfordshire. He died in November 1998.

PART 4 *THE LEGACY*

Rugby tours do not end when the players arrive home and go their separate ways to their families and homes or to their places of work and local clubs. The immediate post-script to the great adventure of the Young Dragons was more unusual than most. Having arrived back in Southampton on Friday 14 September 1956, the following Monday saw a dozen of them return to school and eight of them packing their bags again in readiness for their first term at university . The remaining eight, however, experienced what was surely the ultimate change of environment after a fortnight on a cruise liner – they reported for National Service. In the years that followed there would be other diversionary paths in their professional careers. Sixteen qualified as teachers, one became a professional cricketer, a couple excelled at scientific research and development, two more in marketing, and among the others there was an accountant, vet, toolmaker and dentist. As rugby players, several of those who returned to school also won further caps for the Welsh Secondary Schools in the next one, two or even three years, there were representatives in the high profile inter-services' matches at Twickenham, one played in the Varsity Match, nearly everyone gave great service to first-class clubs in Wales and a few also did so in England, a couple tried their hand at rugby league, and two played senior international rugby. And the friendships that were strengthened in South Africa lived – and live on – in the regular informal get-togethers and more organised reunions that have ensured the survival of the Young Dragons as a group half-a-century later.

Along the way, other legacies of their achievements in 1956 and their ambitions nurtured then have emerged. One of the most significant must be the influence of these young players as they grew older as coaches in their own right. The many teachers inevitably were important in their individual schools as they not only taught and coached but also encouraged that vital ingredient of young rugby culture, the Saturday morning matches. Others went to their local clubs and fostered mini-rugby. On other levels they have also provided expertise in senior representative rugby. The role of Clive Rowlands as the national team coach of Wales, the highest possible profile in the Principality, needs no introduction. Suffice to say that in his years in charge he helped deliver Triple Crowns, Grand Slams and international championship titles as well as a brand of rugby that became synonymous with national identity. But there were triumphs and distinguished service elsewhere, too: Leighton Davies with generations of college students passing through Cardiff; Jack Davies with the Welsh Youth Rugby Union; and, perhaps most significant of all, John Elgar Williams, who in the best part of 30 years as an executive member of the reconstituted Welsh Schools' Rugby Union (Senior Group), served successively as chairman, secretary, coach and president.

There were administrators in other spheres as well. T Rowley Jones continued to serve for many years as honorary secretary of the secondary schools, a cause unashamedly closest to his heart, and then became president of the Welsh Rugby Union in 1977-78; Clive Rowlands emulated the latter achievement in 1989-90, the season after he had managed the successful British Isles team in Australia. Brian Skirrow became an unsung hero at the International Rugby Board, organising as Tournament Director vital elements of the sensationally successful 1995 Rugby World Cup Finals in South Africa.

The list of legacies is endless. Yet what remains as perhaps the most enduring of all is the pioneering element of 1956. It is worth repeating that before then no representative Welsh team of any age group had ventured beyond Europe on a rugby tour. And after 1956 it would be another eight years before the next team, the senior Wales XV captained by Clive Rowlands, returned to South Africa or anywhere else south of the equator.

By the 1980s the Welsh Schools (Senior Group) were also contemplating tours to the far flung corners of the rugby world. Canada, Zimbabwe and, eventually, New Zealand and Australia were earmarked as possible destinations. Just as T Rowley Jones had been a driving force in the 1950s, so now John Elgar Williams was a visionary and leading figure. He left no one in doubt when he wrote: 'To a young 18 year old who had hardly crossed Offa's Dyke, let alone gone abroad, my selection for the tour of the Young Dragons was the greatest thrill of my life. I returned after those two months a more assured and confident young man, and with a burning desire that if the opportunity ever arose in the future I would provide the young players of Wales with a similar experience.'

His mentors back in 1956 would have approved – but they would in no way have been surprised. As the Young Dragons returned home, Ned Gribble was already preparing his official report to the rest of the executive committee. He concluded: 'The sincere thanks of everyone goes to this happy team of boys who so nobly upheld the fine tradition of Welsh rugby football. They left this country unheralded and almost unnoticed, but returned as worthy ambassadors of Cymru Fach and a credit to the schools of our beloved Wales.' They were, truly, the Dragons Who Roared.

Old friends reunited again at the 40th anniversary dinner in Cardiff in 1996.

A PERSONAL MEMOIR

By Maurice Palmer

The tour gave me a true perspective of what distance was all about. Coming from Pembrokeshire 'a long way' was to travel to Cardiff or London. To travel to the limit of my existing experience to reach the embarkation point for a two week sea voyage and then, having completed that, to travel 39 hours by train in South Africa and still be in the Cape Province was, to say the least, stretching my imagination. (From Llangwm to Lesotho in three easy stages!!)

Throughout the trip I was, and I think the whole team were, conscious of following in the footsteps of a very successful Lions team which had a strong core of Welsh players. The standing of Welsh rugby in South Africa was high and we were desperate not to debase the currency.

A further lasting impression was the sight of Table Mountain emerging out of the early morning mist as we made our approach to Cape Town, a city which I believe to be one of the most beautiful in the world.

The people were wonderfully hospitable. Nothing appeared to be too much trouble and they looked after us and entertained us in fine style. Their life-style appeared to be something which few of us had been exposed to before and they were determined that we left South Africa with a warm feeling for the country and its people – which we undoubtedly did.

The one issue, which I found very difficult to reconcile, was the imposition of the apartheid regime by an overtly religious nation. The whole concept of apartheid was alien to my upbringing of socialism and chapel and left a very uneasy feeling about the politics of the country. However, having been warned that 'we were guests in someone else's country' it was something that I put to one side and got on with enjoying the experience of travelling and playing rugby. Nevertheless, once the tour was over and the euphoria was diminishing I was able to form a more rational and studied view of the situation and my concerns regarding the system intensified.

With hindsight, the rugby was intense but got easier as the tour progressed, both for the team and for me as an individual, as we gained in confidence. The power of the team ethic was powerfully demonstrated. Our fitness levels were higher than any of us had previously experienced, but the training was also probably very necessary to keep in check the potential ravages of a dietary intake to which none of us had been previously accustomed. Team spirit was excellent throughout and I have no recollection of any internal bickering or even cross words.

With regard to the contrast in playing styles of our opponents the most relevant to me were the different roles played by the back row forwards in South Africa which made the task of the scrum half that much more difficult. Both wing-forwards (flankers) focused their attention on the scrum-half with the lock (no 8) concentrating on the fly-half. This was a feature of South African play which was confirmed and emphasised in discussions with Dickie Jeeps of the afore mentioned Lions tour.

The highlight of the tour had to be playing in a team at the top of its form and winning at

Ellis Park in front of around 20,000 spectators against what should have been the strongest opposition. It was the point at which the tour was deemed to be a success and we all felt the better for that. I think the management relaxed a little bit at this point and we all enjoyed the moment and indeed the remainder of the tour.

As far as what one gained from the tour, one can certainly say that it was twenty-seven long-standing friends. The still obvious camaraderie after all these years is very noticeable to anyone unfortunate enough to be in our combined company. In my case it gave me a great deal of self-confidence, which I hope was not misplaced, both in a rugby and social sense. Going to college I knew that I could be self sufficient for eight weeks at a time, which many of my contemporaries straight from school struggled with. I think also it served to confirm the work ethic, so espoused by Welsh parents, that hard work, fitness and team work could overcome many natural disadvantages both on and off the rugby field.

In essence, it was a huge privilege to be part of a ground breaking, successful tour and I will be forever grateful for that opportunity and to those people who had the foresight and the energy to make it possible.

David and Heather Walkey with Maurice Palmer at a Young Dragons' reunion in the Celtic Manor Hotel, Newport, in July 2003.

POST SCRIPT

I was clearing out my parents' home in the autumn of 2005 and came across the memorabilia of my father, T Rowley Jones, a former president of the Welsh Rugby Union who was also the long-standing secretary of the Welsh Secondary Schools Rugby Union (WSSRU). I knew of course that this memorabilia existed; it was the result of a lifetime of involvement in rugby union football – programmes, dinner menus, correspondence, ties, badges, etc, much of which pre-dated the second war. Amongst this collection was a particularly extensive archive of correspondence, diaries, scrap books and even cine film of the 1956 Welsh Secondary Schools tour to South Africa – The Young Dragons. As I sifted through this material, it occurred to me that 2006 was the 50th anniversary of the tour and how appropriate it would be to mark the occasion with the publication of a book. By a somewhat circuitous route I met Alan Evans who had written previously about the Young Dragons and I am indebted to him for taking on the task and producing such a splendid result.

The Young Dragons tour to South Africa in 1956 was, it turns out, a milestone in the history of rugby union football as it was the first tour ever undertaken by a national team to the southern hemisphere, pre-dating the first senior tour, by the Scottish national side, to South Africa in 1960. When he set about organising the tour the motivation of my father was certainly not to establish his place in the annals of rugby history. It was more straightforward. He was totally committed to Welsh secondary schools rugby, something I took for granted at the time but now, as I look back, it is clear he had drive, vision and enthusiasm that are not often encountered. When I hired people into the company I started in the early 1990s, I looked for energy, vision, determination and single-mindedness: I would have hired my father – even though he would have been a management challenge!

My father felt very strongly that team games should flourish in schools, that involvement in a team built a sense of responsibility, a sense of purpose and engendered a sense of loyalty to one's fellow team members and one's school; values that do not seem as prevalent today. It is clear from reading this book that the young men who went on the tour were inspired by these values which have played an important role in the shaping of their lives.

It took his drive and determination to get the tour off the ground. At the time he was the assistant secretary of the WSSRU and when the Union received an approach from Levi Jones, a Welsh-born teacher living in South Africa, for a Welsh tour to that country it was apparently dismissed as a rather fanciful notion. I cannot vouch for the committee discussions that took place but my father subsequently told me that he was instructed 'to go away and play'! This was exactly the right stimulus for his rather obstinate streak to assume even greater importance in his persona. There was nothing he liked more than to be right – it's clearly genetic – and on this occasion to prove that a whole committee was wrong and he was right, was too good an opportunity to miss. You will have read that the South African schools' tour to Wales in 1955 unexpectedly generated a significant profit so this gave the doubters on the committee some encouragement, although I know from my own personal memories that there were still many reservations.

As a boy, still at primary school, I remember quite clearly the planning and meticulous preparation for the tour. The dining room at the family home in Brynmawr was the nerve centre and my mother, Mary, now in her 90th year, was a very willing and able personal assistant. She obviously wielded considerable power, judging by the number of times her signature appears on various documents in the archive of information which underpins this book!

Apart from the logistics of the tour there was the small matter of raising up to £3,000, a daunting sum even by today's standards. The approach was simple; my parents went through the telephone directory and mailed over 8,000 letters asking for financial help. My mother recalls that donations of all sizes were received, the smallest she can remember was around five shillings and the largest £100. It was ironic that the latter was from Cardiff City Football Club who donated substantially more than the Welsh Rugby Union.

In addition there were other fund raising activities undertaken by various people around the country together with one further activity organised at the Brynmawr HQ – a raffle. As far as I remember, the prizes were autographed rugby balls but, judging by the number of tickets sold, these were much sought after. For weeks it seemed, ticket stubs arrived at the house and these were all folded and stored in what can only be described as medium sized oil drums from which the draw was made. During that time anybody who came to the house was given a pile of stubs and told to get folding. My mother tells me that my father even coerced some of the prefects at Brynmawr Grammar School into helping.

It became clear that the tour was no longer a pipe dream and then the jockeying for a place on the tour started. There were 28 boys, selected by an almost endless series of trial matches – I remember this myself some years later – but there were also to be six teachers and most of the candidates were far too old to take part in trials! It is funny how certain things stick in one's mind but I vividly remember a conversation that took place in the winter of 1955/56 between my father and one of the more senior members of the WSSRU committee. I would often go with my father to trial matches on a Saturday and on this particular occasion I was in the back of the car returning from a match, with my father and the aforementioned senior member in the front. It was put to my father that, in spite of the fact that he had taken on the lion's share of the organisation, he was considered too junior by some factions of the committee to be on the tour itself. I remember the silence in the car, always a bad sign as far as he was concerned, as he digested the implication of this remark. Fortunately common sense, not to mention fair play, prevailed I am sure aided by some 'diplomacy' from my father.

I can remember hearing bits about the tour and receiving the old blue airmail letters from my father. I recall the farmer at Whitlow Farm in Saundersfoot, where our caravan was parked, running across the field one day brandishing one of these letters, curious to know the reason for someone receiving a communication sent by air! My clear memory however is going with my mother to meet my father on his return at Newport station on a gloriously sunny day and hearing him give a radio interview on the platform to the BBC. I was a very proud 9-year-old boy. I asked my mother recently whether she missed my father during this period, 'Of course' she said, 'the car had a slow puncture the whole time he was away!'

I hope you have enjoyed reading this fascinating book. There were clearly many people involved in the historic 1956 Young Dragons tour to South Africa and this book is a tribute to them all. It has been my pleasure to be involved in some small way in its production.

David Rowley Jones
Ashwell, Herts, June 2006

ACKNOWLEDGEMENTS

This book would not have been possible without the co-operation, encouragement and sheer enthusiasm of every one of the 28 Young Dragons or their families. Of the 22 survivors, four now live overseas in locations as far apart as Alicante and Arizona but distance proved no obstacle to sharing knowledge and anecdotes as modern communications kicked in. Closer to home personal interviews, which invariably stretched far beyond their intended time slot, were an absolute joy. So, too, were the lunches and overnight stays as more and more memories flooded back. Sadly, six of the players have passed away in the intervening years but, again, their widows have been incredibly helpful in answering questions and providing mementoes that were understandably tinged with sadness. I thank everyone for their hospitality - and also their patience as husbands apparently disappeared into the depths of lofts, attics and garages in search of scrapbooks, photographs and other documentation that in some cases had not seen the light of day for decades. I can assure them that their diligence was worthwhile.

Five of the six teachers have died and Gwynfor Davies still lives in Staffordshire. His tour journals and that of T Rowley Jones have been essential sources of information - and, it has to be said, wonderful testimony to the agreeable habit of diary writing of an increasingly bygone age. Rowley's family have been particularly crucial to this entire project. His son, David, sowed the seeds of the idea as the fiftieth anniversary year of the Young Dragons dawned and then went on to underwrite the costs of the book. The Wooden Spoon Society, the rugby charity supporting disadvantaged children and young people, will benefit from much of its profit. Rowley's widow, Mary, who was at his side throughout the inspirational fund-raising process that made the tour viable (and apparently signed most of the receipts if not the cheques!), still lives near David in Hertfordshire. As anticipated, an afternoon spent in her company filled in all sorts of missing information and was also a reminder, inadvertently so on her part, of just why these young pioneers deserved to have their tour and its legacy recorded for posterity.

Several other individuals and organisations have played a part in the project. In the early days Dai Richards of the World Rugby Museum provided great encouragement, then Isabel Butcher of 'Designis' was invaluable in providing technical expertise in the production of the illustrations and also designing the cover, and, as the finishing line approached, Pît Dafis and his colleagues at Gomer Press ensured that the book was published on time. The president of the Welsh Rugby Union, Keith Rowlands, who played for the Welsh Secondary Schools in 1955 and so was unfortunate to miss the tour by a year, has kindly written the Foreword.

David Rowley Jones and myself also wish to thank Bob Harris and the Wooden Spoon Society for their interest and their future involvement in promoting the book.

Alan Evans
Cardiff, June 2006

APPENDIX

1. The Young Dragons Tour Party

	Name	School	Position	DoB	Ht	Wt
1	I Jones	Llanelli GS	Full Back	28.6.37	5.7	10.11
2	J L Ebsworth	Pembroke GS	Wing	22.4.38	5.10	11.3
3	D M Johnston	HMS Conway	Centre	14.11.37	5.11	11.11
4	R D Thomas	Neath GS	Centre	7.6.37	5.10	11.10
5	T E Evans	Caerphilly GS	Wing	6.10.38	5.9	11.10
6	A H M Rees	Glan Afan GS	Fly-Half	17.2.38	5.6	10.8
7	H F Merrick	Cathays HS	Scrum-Half	11.8.37	5.8	11.6
8	D G A Walkey	Bassaleg GS	Prop	29.11.37	5.10	13.7
9	D J Jones	Mountain Ash GS	Hooker	5.4.38	5.9	12.7
10	M H H Thomas	Tonyrefail GS	Prop	3.1.38	5.11	15.0
11	B Harrison	Grove Park GS	2nd Row	6.5.37	6.1	13.5
12	D J Puddle	Brynmawr GS	2nd Row	23.3.37	5.11	14.0
13	W T A Williams	QueenElizabeth GS	Wing-Forward	22.10.37	5.10	12.6
14	W G Davies	Ebbw Vale GS	Lock	18.8.38	6.3	14.0
15	D L Davies	Garw GS	Wing-Forward	2.6.38	5.8	12.2
16	D T Jones	Caerphilly GS	Full Back	1.3.39	5.11	12.5
17	D C Phillips	Neath GS	Wing	27.7.37	5.10	11.7
18	R Griffiths	Tonypandy GS	Centre	29.10.38	5.10	11.0
19	J E Williams	Amman Valley GS	Centre	8.12.37	5.7	9.9
20	B A Skirrow	Cardiff HS	Wing	24.12.38	6.1	13.0
21	D Robinson	Mountain Ash GS	Fly-Half	2.2.38	5.3	9.7
22	M S Palmer	Haverfordwest GS	Scrum-Half	7.3.39	5.9	11.4
23	D C T Rowlands	Maesydderwen GS	Scrum-Half	14.5.38	5.10	11.12
24	N J Johnson	Bassaleg GS	Prop	9.8.38	5.11	15.0
25	H J Morgan	Llanelli GS	Prop	17.5.38	5.10	13.4
26	J E Davies	Cowbridge GS	2nd Row	5.9.37	6.1	12.11
27	M W Pemberton	Newport HS	Lock	15.3.37	6.2	13.0
28	A Morris	Neath Technical	Hooker	11.3.39	5.11	12.0

Officials

E R Gribble (Tonyrefail GS)
G J Davies (Bridgend GS)
G Davies (Queen Elizabeth GS, Carmarthen)
T Rowley Jones (Brynmawr GS)
P Williams (Abertillery GS)
H S Warrington (Merthyr)

2. Match Record

	Date	Venue	Opponents	R	Points For			Against		
					T C D P	Pts		T C D P	Pts	
1	Aug 7	Port Elizabeth	Eastern Province	L	2 1 1	11		3 2 1 1	19	
2	Aug 11	Bloemfontein	Orange Free State	D	1 1 1	9		1 2	9	
3	Aug 15	Ermelo	Eastern Transvaal Country XV	W	8 3 1	33		1	3	
4	Aug 18	Springs	Eastern Transvaal	W	2 1	8			0	
5	Aug 22	Potchefstroom	Western Transvaal	W	2 1	8		1	3	
6	Aug 25	Johannesburg	Transvaal	W	4 3 1	21		1	3	
7	Aug 27	Kimberley	Griqualand West	W	3 1 1	14		2	6	
8	Aug 29	Wellington	Boland	W	1 1 1	8			0	

Overall Record

Played 8   Won 6   Drew 1   Lost 1
Points for 112 (23 tries, 11 cons, 2 drops, 5 pens); Against 43 (7 tries, 2 cons, 1 drop, 5 pens)

3. Appearances

8 – B Harrison, D G A Walkey
7 – D L Davies, D J Jones, W T A Williams
6 – W G Davies, T E Evans, N J Johnson, D M Johnston, D T Jones
5 – J L Ebsworth, M S Palmer, M W Pemberton, A H M Rees, M H H Thomas,
    R D Thomas
4 – R Griffiths
3 – I Jones, D C Phillips
2 – H F Merrick, D Robinson, D C T Rowlands, B A Skirrow
1 – J E Davies, H J Morgan, A Morris, D J Puddle, J E Williams

4. Points' Scorers

33 – W T A Williams (2 tries, 9 cons, 3 pens)

9 – R Griffiths, B Harrison, D G A Walkey (3 tries each), I Jones (1 drop, 2 pens)

8 – A H M Rees (1 try, 1 drop, 1 con)

6 – T E Evans, D M Johnston, R D Thomas (2 tries each)

3 – D L Davies, J L Ebsworth, M S Palmer, D C Phillips, D C T Rowlands (1 try each)

2 – M W Pemberton (1 con)

Biographical Notes

ALAN EVANS

Alan Evans was originally from the Garw Valley and traces his life long interest in rugby back to the summer of 1956 when his uncle, Gwynfor Davies, returned from South Africa with tales of the Young Dragons and their epic tour. Half a century later, he regards his research and authorship of this book as a way of repaying the debt of inspiration he received then.

After teaching for thirty years in Warwickshire, Alan returned to Cardiff in 1998 and commenced a new career in sports journalism and management. Between 1999 and 2005 he was the media officer for Cardiff Rugby Football Club and then the new regional team, Cardiff Blues. He eventually relinquished the position in order to devote more time to his new honorary appointment as Registrar of the Barbarians, for whom he is the archivist and media officer.

Alan has concurrently fulfilled the responsibility of consultant editor for the International Rugby Hall of Fame, the New Zealand-based trust that inducted its first fifteen players in 1997 and has added more legends of the game every two years since then.

As well as regularly reporting on matches for several newspapers on a freelance basis, he has contributed features celebrating the heritage of the game for magazines, brochures and match programmes.

The Dragons Who Roared is Alan's seventh book. His previous titles are:

> *The Butchers Arms Boys* (with Gareth Harris), Rugby Unlimited, 1997
> *Cardiff Rugby Football Club* 1876-1939 (with Duncan Gardiner), Tempus, 1999
> *Cardiff Rugby Football Club* 1940-2000 (with Duncan Gardiner), Tempus, 2001
> *The Young One* (with David Young), Mainstream, 2001
> *Taming The Tourists*, Vertical Editions, 2003
> *The Barbarians*, The United Nations of Rugby, Mainstream, 2005.

Alan has also contributed to *More Heart and Soul*, (University of Wales Press), a collection of essays celebrating Welsh rugby, and edited *Feat of Clay*, the history of the world of Groggs. He is currently working on a book on the 1950 British Isles tour to Australasia, Lions and Adventurers, to be published by Tempus in October 2006.

DAVID ROWLEY JONES

David Rowley Jones was born in Abergavenny in 1947. He was educated at Brynmawr Grammar School, where he was taught by his father, Selwyn College, Cambridge and Guy's Hospital, London. At school he was always known by his proper name but when he left Wales he was immediately christened 'Dai', to the chagrin of his mother.

Dai qualified in medicine in 1971 and became a Member of the Royal College of Physicians in 1977. After being a house surgeon at Guy's he worked as a house physician and senior house officer at Nevill Hall Hospital, Abergavenny and subsequently at the University of Wales Hospital in Cardiff on the Professorial Medical Unit. He pursued a career in the pharmaceutical industry, initially with Smith, Kline and French Ltd, where he was elected to the Board in 1987, and then with SmithKline Beecham, becoming Senior Vice-President for Worldwide Marketing. He left in 1994 and founded a company, Athena Neurosciences Europe Ltd, which was acquired by the Elan Corporation of Ireland for whom he established a European business, leaving in 2001. He then founded Daffodil Consulting LLP and has been on the Board of a number of companies, including English Sinfonia, a professional orchestra.

At school, Dai (David in those days) represented Monmouthshire and Mid-Wales at rugby, Breconshire and Radnorshire at athletics and South Wales (there was no junior Welsh team at that time) at golf. He was a Cambridge 'blue' and a London University 'purple' at golf and played for Monmouthshire in the Channel League. He is a former captain of Royal Worlington and Newmarket Golf Club and a member of The Royal and Ancient Golf Club of St Andrews. He was also an accomplished squash player, playing in the top county league in both Hertfordshire and Cambridgeshire.

Dai lives in Hertfordshire with his wife Sue and they have four grown up daughters and three grandchildren. Their youngest daughter, Emily, is a professional singer and maintains the Welsh connection by appearing regularly with the London Welsh Male Voice Choir as their soloist.

KEITH ROWLANDS

Keith Rowlands became the 47th president of the Welsh Rugby Union in the autumn of 2004. His election was the culmination of a distinguished career as a player, administrator and figure-head in both Welsh and world rugby.

Keith was born in Brithdir and educated in the grammar schools of Cowbridge and Aberdare. It was while he was a student at the latter that he won his Welsh Secondary Schools' cap against England at Cardiff Arms Park in April, 1955. In the same team were future Young Dragons Rhys Thomas, Alan Rees and Allan Williams. By the time the tour to South Africa came around a year later, Keith had left school to study at London University. He played senior rugby as a number 8 and lock for Aberaman, London Welsh and Llanelli before joining Cardiff in 1961. He went on to captain the Arms Park club for two seasons and lead them to victory over the touring Wallabies in 1966. Keith played five times for Wales and toured South Africa with the Lions in 1962, when he played in 18 of the 25 matches, including three tests. He scored a try in the fourth test against the Springboks, but, controversially, an earlier effort in the second test at Durban was disallowed by the South African referee; the British Isles lost the match 3-nil.

When his playing career ended prematurely after suffering a broken leg on New Year's Eve, 1966, Keith turned to committee work for Cardiff, eventually becoming club chairman and a WRU district representative. He joined the International Rugby Board in 1981/82 and was appointed its secretary in 1988. When he retired from the post in 1996 he was invited to manage the organisation of the 1999 Rugby World Cup in Wales.

THE ORGANIC HANDBOOK 2

PESTS

How to control the
on fruit and vegetables

REVISED EDITION

Pauline Pears and Bob Sherman

Henry Doubleday Research Association / Search Press

The authors would like to thank
Lawrence D. Hills, founder and president of the
HDRA and a guiding light to many an organic
gardener.

First Published in Great Britain 1990
Search Press Ltd.,
Wellwood, North Farm Road,
Tunbridge Wells, Kent TN2 3DR

in association with

The Henry Doubleday Research Association,
National Centre for Organic Gardening,
Ryton-on-Dunsmore,
Coventry, CV8 3LG

Revised edition 1992

Reprinted 2000

Illustrations by Polly Pinder
Photographs by Charlotte de la Bedoyére
All the photographs in this book have been
taken in organic gardens, and all of the fruit,
vegetables and flowers pictured have been
grown organically.

The publishers would like to thank the following
for allowing them to photograph their animals:
The Burstow Wildlife Sanctuary for the
hedgehog and the jay which appear on pages 3
and 21 respectively; Mrs. H.A.C.T Clark for the
bat which appears on page 12; Mrs. Nicky
Edwards of The Wise Owl Pet Shop for the
rabbit which appears on page 24.

The publishers would also like to thank Andrew
Halstead for his help in the preparation of this
book.

ISBN 0 85532 741 3

Printed in Spain by Elkar S. Coop, Bilbao

Conversion chart

From centimetres to inches		From grams to ounces	
1 cm	= ½ in	7 g	= ¼ oz
2.5 cm	= 1 in	14 g	= ½ oz
5 cm	= 2 in	28 g	= 1 oz
10 cm	= 4 in	110 g	= 4 oz
50 cm	= 20 in		
100 cm (1 m)	= 40 in	From litres to pints	
1 sq m	= 1.2 sq yds	1 l	= 1.75 pt

Exact conversions from imperial to metric measures are
not possible, so the metric measures have been rounded
up.

Note referring to the scale of the pictures

The actual size as shown with some of the pictures is
approximate only, as some of the creatures do in fact
vary in size quite considerably.

Introduction

The obvious way of dealing with pests organically is to swap a chemical spray for one that is called 'organic'. But, although the 'organic' sprays may be safer than some, they are certainly not harmless and should never be seen as the mainstay of any pest control strategy. There is a whole range of effective alternatives, techniques and tricks that can be used to keep pests in check which do not rely on the use of sprays.

There are, for example, ways of making your garden more attractive to the beneficial creatures that are natural pest controllers. Also, organic methods of soil care result in vigorous, well-balanced plants which will be less attractive to pests and diseases; so this enables the plants to resist attack.

When and how to sow and plant are important factors in ensuring that plants grow without any problems. Pest build-up can be minimized by crop rotation and good hygiene, and pests kept at bay by the use of barriers and traps.

Success with any form of pest control is improved if the problem is first correctly identified. Although it is difficult to cause much harm by using the wrong method of organic control, a lot of time and effort can be wasted in trying to control the wrong pest! The charts on pages 40–43 will help you with the identification process.

The organic gardener should never aim to wipe out every pest (what a Herculean task that would be!), but just aim only to reduce pests to an acceptable level. Learning more about the pests in your garden, either by reading and/ or observation, will help to prevent panic. You will soon learn how much damage plants can tolerate without being harmed. The presence of a pest does *not* necessarily mean that it is going to be a problem.

The best way to achieve an acceptable level of pest control is to use a combination of several of the techniques covered in this book. The pesticides that are permissable for use in an organic garden are described at the end of the book, but their use should be kept to a minimum, as they can harm creatures other than the pests at which they are aimed. Also, whenever a spray has to be used, the gardener should be looking for ways to avoid the problem arising in future seasons.

The much loved hedgehog should be encouraged to stay in your garden to feast on slugs.

Know and encourage your friends

Take a stroll around your garden and you'll soon notice all sorts of tiny creatures going about their business. The more you look, the more you will see . . . .

At this stage it is all too easy to assume that these creatures are hell–bent on eating your favourite plants. Most of us have been brought up to regard anything that creeps, crawls, wriggles or squirms as something 'nasty'. In fact most of the creatures in your garden are harmless and even useful. They are working hard to prevent pests and diseases from getting out of hand.

Every pest and disease has its own predatory pest and disease. If this were not so, we would be crawling with caterpillars and knee deep in greenfly. The aim in an organic garden is to help these 'beneficial' creatures in their work and to try and tip the balance in their favour. The first step is to stop using chemical sprays that can harm them. In the past, creatures have actually been turned into pests as a result of sprays killing off their natural enemies. The fruit tree red spider mite *Panonychus ulmi*, for example, was not a pest until the 1920's, when tar oil winter washes and other sprays were introduced. Until then, mite numbers had been kept down by a host of natural enemies including lacewings, capsids, beetles and predatory mites. The winter washes killed these natural enemies, but allowed the red spider mite to breed unchecked, reaching levels which made it a serious pest. Other insecticides only compounded the problem. This is a well-documented example of pesticides actually creating pest problems, but there are surely many more which have not yet been studied.

The second step in helping our garden friends is to get to know them (so they are not killed in error) and to keep them happy by supplying them with suitable sources of food and shelter.

We cannot always rely on these natural creatures to keep pests down to the levels we would like, but they play a significant part and we would be lost without them. This chapter introduces some of our 'garden friends' – from mites, insects, and beetles to frogs, lizards and birds, and suggests ways we can encourage them to live and work in our gardens.

Identifying garden friends

The ladybird is one of the best known of our garden friends. Both adults and developing larvae do a useful job in eating greenfly and other aphids, scale insects, mealy-bugs, thrips and mites. Adult ladybirds hibernate in winter and have to start eating soon after they wake in spring. A clump of nettles can provide a useful early breakfast, as nettle aphids, which do not trouble other plants, are one of the earliest to appear.

Actual size × 14

Actual size ×9

Ladybirds

The red and black adult ladybird below (Coccinella 7-punctata) is much too pretty for anyone to take for a pest, but the slaty–blue crawling larvae above are not always so lucky, and can cause alarm when they appear in numbers on garden plants. Top right is a ladybird pupa (a stage between larva and adult).

There are many kinds of ladybirds including red ones with only two spots, black ones with red spots and, as illustrated on page 4, yellow ones with black spots (Propylea 14-punctata).

Actual size ×11

Hover-fly Syrphus ribesii

Actual size ×9

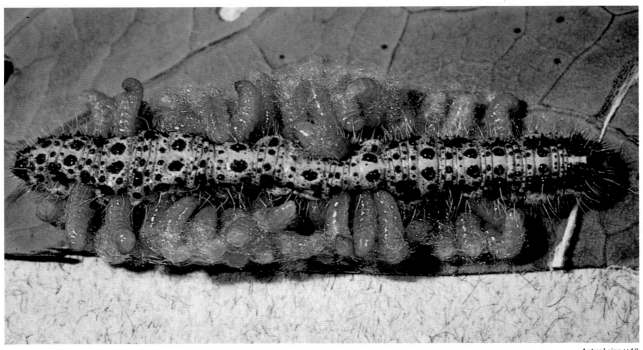

Actual size ×10

Parasitic wasps
The larvae of the parasitic wasp Cotesias glomerata *emerging from a large white caterpillar.*

6

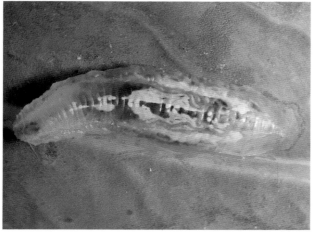

Actual size × 7

Hover-fly
On page 6 is Syrphus ribesii, *one of the many hover-fly species. Hover-flies have flatter bodies and tend to be smaller than wasps. They all hover silently and do not sting! The adults feed on pollen and nectar while the larvae (above) are the ones that eat aphids and other small pests. The larvae can also be green.*

Another attractive 'friendly' insect is the hover-fly. Unfortunately it is often mistaken for a wasp (*see page 26*), but once you get to know them the difference is easily spotted. Hover-fly larvae are not difficult to find; you only have to look amongst a colony of aphids. Just one larva can eat one aphid per minute!

The more adult hover-flies eat, the more eggs they lay, so it is worth providing them with a good supply of food. They will take nectar and pollen from a whole range of flat, open, single flowers, such as *Limnanthes douglasii* (the poached egg plant), *Convolvulus tricolor*, fennel, buckwheat and many others, (*see page 13*).

There is also an abundance of parasitic wasps and flies in the garden that kill a whole range of pests including aphids, caterpillars, scale insects, root fly larvae and whitefly. Parasitic wasps *Aphidius* are tiny and rarely noticed, but the damage they do to pests can easily be seen.

Another common sight, later in the season, is a large white cabbage caterpillar, surrounded by yellow, almost fluffy looking cocoons. These are the young of another parasitic wasp, *Cotesias glomerata*, which have been living and feeding within the caterpillar.

Actual size × 3

Aphid shells
If you look at a colony of aphids, you may see some straw-coloured 'shells' with a small hole, as above. This is a sure sign that tiny parasitic wasps (Aphidius), shown below, have been at work. They lay their eggs inside the aphids where the young live, then grow until they are ready to cut their way out, leaving hapless, dead aphids in their wake. The picture above shows both live and dead aphids.

Actual size × 6

Lacewing

There are several types of lacewings, so-called because of their beautiful 'gauze-like' wings which are green or fawn. The ones pictured here are Chrysopa septempunctata.

Actual size ×6

Earwig

Many people shudder at the sight of earwigs (Forficulidae). They are often automatically 'squashed' as a pest despite the fact that they eat codling moth eggs and woolly aphids. Earwigs can be mild pests but their good points outweigh their bad.

Actual size ×5

All these tiny wasps and flies are attracted to the flat flowers of the *Umbellifer* family, such as carrots, parsnips and fennel. They also like the *Compositae* (daisy-type) flowers which include Michaelmas daisies, mustard and yarrow. The *Compositae* also provide nectar and pollen for the delicate lacewing, whose voracious larvae feed on aphids and other soft-bodied creatures. The adults enjoy a few insects too, but they need a supply of pollen, especially when laying eggs.

Earwigs and ground and rove beetles, the large black scuttly ones, are also useful. Ground and rove beetles are shy creatures who appreciate a garden with lots of cover, such as thick leaf or bark mulches, ground cover plants etc. They will be rare in a garden where the soil is bare, every last scrap of vegetation cleared away, and the grass scalped to a bowling-green.

Rove beetles

There are many different rove beetles (Staphylinidae), mostly black and brown in various sizes. All are shy and fast moving and can be seen easily at night. They enjoy slugs, root aphids, root fly larvae, other pests and their eggs.

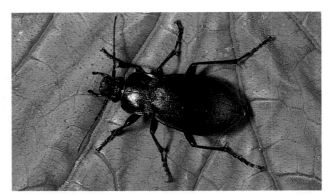

Ground beetles

There are large numbers of ground beetles (Carabidae). They vary in size from 5 to 25 mm, and they are predators of many garden pests, including slugs.

Anthocorid bug

There are many varieties of anthocorid bugs. The one below is Anthocoris nemorum, *one of the smallest. There are brown and black ones, and they are important predators of fruit and vegetable pests: aphids, root aphids, capsid bugs, caterpillars, midges, blossom weevils and red spider mite.*

Centipedes, not to be confused with millipedes, also appreciate a mulch to hide in while they rest between meals of slugs and other pests. A little bit of studied 'untidiness' will make a garden much more attractive to many useful creatures.

Centipedes

These creatures are 'friends' unlike the millipede in the bottom picture, which is a nuisance, (see also page 24). There are various varieties of centipedes which have only one pair of legs per segment, whilst millipedes have two.

Actual size ×4

Actual size ×4

Actual size ×4

Frogs and toads
Frogs (top right) eat slugs, and toads (below right) account for large numbers of insects, that is if you are lucky enough to have them in your garden.

Garden ponds are becoming popular in these conservation conscious days, which can only be a good thing. They may be responsible for the current frog population, which remains relatively healthy despite the fact that there has been a vast reduction in the number of ponds in the countryside. Lucky is the gardener who can attract slug-eating frogs to live and breed in the pond.

Hedgehogs seem to be much more popular than frogs, having a 'cuddly' image – despite the fact that they are unpleasant to hug! They are welcome in the garden as yet another slug-eater. Encourage one to stay by providing a hibernating site like a pile of logs or autumn leaves under a hedge, or even a custom-built hedgehog box.

Someone else who appreciates somewhere to hide is the slow-worm. These snake-like creatures are in fact legless lizards and are totally harmless to humans – but not to slugs!

Slow-worm
These creatures are often mistaken for snakes and are now not a common sight. They should be encouraged, as slugs form a principle part of their diet. They can grow up to 50 cm long.

Although some birds can be a nuisance in the garden, many are extremely valuable and should be encouraged. Nesting boxes and fat on a string when food is scarce may encourage blue tits to make their home with you. These busy birds are experts at winkling out codling moth cocoons in winter and aphid eggs from the gnarled bits of apple tree bark. They can account for ninety-five per cent of codling moth cocoons. When digging a plot where pests are overwintering, robins and other birds are always welcome. Their eagle eyes soon spot a tasty morsel, which they are quick to seize upon.

It may be difficult to regard spiders with affection, but they should be seen as welcome guests. Many species living in orchards and gardens are useful predators, and they are always more abundant on unsprayed sites. Different species of spider will vary in their diet, but this can include spider mites, aphids, codling moths, winter moths and their larvae, leafhoppers, midges and other small insect pests.

Bats

These creatures, hunted almost to extinction in the past due to their association with horror vampire stories, are now a protected species in many parts of the world. Bats will eat up to 3,500 insects in one night, so it is worth encouraging them to stay.

Actual size ×8

Glow-worm (Lampyris noctiluca)
The glow-worm is a creature associated with old pastures and woodland edges. Changes in land use, with consequent loss of habitat, mean that they are now fairly rare. The picture shows the male larva, which does not glow as brightly as the female, but both live on slugs and snails.

The beneficial creatures introduced here are just a few of many that can be found in nature. Make your garden a friendly place for wildlife and it will repay you handsomely. Not only will pests and diseases diminish, but the garden will be a nicer place to be.

So, next time a creepy–crawly scuttles across your path, don't squash it – it could be a friend.

Plants for attracting and feeding wildlife

The lists on this page show some of the many plants that can attract and feed wildlife, including our garden friends. Some have flowers that provide food in the form of nectar and pollen. Others, such as wild cherry and hawthorn, will provide a supply of 'pests' to keep the beneficials going when none are available elsewhere in the garden.

The annuals are easy to grow in and around the vegetable plot, as well as in flower beds.

The wild flowers and perennials could be introduced into a herb bed, ornamental border or 'wild area' as appropriate. It is not perhaps usual to grow flowers amongst fruit trees and bushes, but a bed with, say, a spring planting of ordinary carrot and parsnip roots could be very beneficial, as well as attractive.

Many gardens are too small to accommodate trees and large shrubs, but there might well be room for a few grown as a hedge.

Whatever the size of your garden, there should be room in it for at least a few 'attractant' plants which will help keep pest levels down and look attractive too.

A – annual   HA – hardy annual   HHA – half-hardy annual   B – biennial   P – perennial

TREES AND SHRUBS

Wild cherry *Prunus avium*		April
Bird cherry *Prunus padus*		May
Wild crab apple *Malus sylvestris*		May
Rowan *Sorbus aucuparia*		May
Hawthorn *Crataegus monogyna*		May
Buckthorn *Rhamnus cathartica*		May/June
Blackthorn *Prunus spinosa*		March/April
False acacia *Robinia pseudoacacia*		June
Mock orange *Philadelphus coronarius*		June/July
Willow *Salix* spp.		March onwards
Guelder rose *Viburnum opulus*		May/June
Spindle *Euonymus europaea*		May/June
Spiraea *Spiraea* spp.		May–July

WILDFLOWERS AND 'WEEDS'

Meadow clary *Salvia pratensis*	P	June-July
Dandelion *Taraxacum officinale*	P	April–June
Clover *Trifolium* spp.	P	May-Oct
Cow parsley *Anthriscus sylvestris*	P	April–June
Nettles *Urtica* spp.	P	May–Sept
Wild strawberry *Fragaria vesca*	P	April–July
Hawksbeard *Crepis biennis*	B	May–July
Sea holly *Eryngium maritimum*	P	July/Aug
Yarrow *Achillea millefolium*	P	June–Nov

Sainfoin *Onobrychis viciifolia*	P	May–Sept

Cultivated relatives of this list should also act as attractants, unless they are highly bred 'double' forms.

CULTIVATED ANNUALS

Poached egg plant *Limnanthes douglasii*	HA
Cornflower *Centaurea cyanus*	HA
Viper's bugloss *Echium vulgare*	HA
Californian poppy *Eschscholzia* spp.	HA
Buckwheat *Fagopyrum esculentum*	HHA
Annual convolvulus *Convolvulus tricolor*	HHA

The flowering period of these plants will vary with sowing time. Hardy annuals can be sown in the autumn to produce flowers early in the following spring.

The wild relatives of these cultivated species may also be grown as attractant plants.

CULTIVATED PERENNIALS

Angelica *Angelica archangelica*	July/Aug
Fennel *Foeniculum vulgare*	July–Sept
Michaelmas daisy *Aster* spp.	Aug–Nov
Shasta daisy *Chrysanthemum maximum*	July–Sept
Golden rod *Solidago* spp.	July–Sept
Pearl everlasting *Anaphalis* spp.	August
Globe thistle *Echinops* spp.	July/Aug

VEGETABLES

Carrot *Daucus carota*	B	June-Aug
Parsnip *Pastinaca sativa*	B	June-Aug

Avoid problems

Get the soil right

The previous chapter concentrates on ways to improve the environment *above* ground. It is equally important to look at the environment *below* ground – i.e. the soil, which is where a large part of most plants grow.

The aim is to create soil conditions which encourage unchecked, balanced plant growth. Plants grown in such conditions will be less attractive to pests and diseases, and more able to resist attack.

The physical conditions

It is unreasonable to expect a plant to grow healthily in a soil that is waterlogged, hard as a rock, or bone dry. A good soil is the basis of effective organic growing, so it is essential to take some time and trouble either to improve the physical conditions of a poor soil, or maintain the quality of a good soil.

Organic manures and composts will help considerably, finally resulting in a soil that is crumbly enough for roots to grow through without difficulty, yet still able to hold sufficient water. Our first handbook *How to make your Garden Fertile* gives a detailed guide to making and using compost, and other organic materials that will help to create a good soil. Good management techniques are also important, such as not working soil that is too wet or too dry, and avoiding excessive digging.

Even organic materials cannot solve severe drainage problems however, which should be sorted out beforehand. This information can be found in good general gardening books.

A good diet

Chemical fertilizers dissolve quickly in the soil which means that a plant can over-feed. Where too much nitrogen is available, the result may be lush, sappy growth, which is just what pests and diseases like. The food contained in organic fertilizers and manures, on the other hand, is only slowly available to the plant, as the materials must first be broken down by the living organisms in the soil. The resulting plants are sturdier and 'harder' and less attractive to pests.

If you are starting a garden from scratch, it is worth having the soil tested to find out whether the pH (acid/alkaline balance) is reasonable for what you want to grow, and that the soil is not lacking in any particular mineral. If necessary, shortfalls can be made up using rock minerals and other organic fertilizers. This is particularly important when planting fruit trees and bushes, which will be in the same site for a long time. It is difficult to correct a deficiency once the ground has been planted up.

Shifting the balance

Just as pests and diseases above ground have their enemies, so do those living in the soil. These are often on a microscopic scale. Anything you do to improve the soil for growing plants will also encourage these natural pest controllers. They appreciate a soil rich in organic matter, and one where harmful soil insecticides are not used.

A good start

Seedlings and young plants are very vulnerable, especially when weather and soil conditions mean that growth is slow. To avoid disaster at this stage, do everything possible to encourage quick emergence and growth.

For example: wait till the soil warms up, or warm it with cloches before sowing. Later sowings will often overtake earlier ones anyway. If the soil tends to set hard, cover seed drills with compost, leaf mould or even a peat/sand mix. This will allow seedlings to come through quickly. Germinating seeds before sowing (pregermination) can also speed up seedling growth.

Raising seedlings indoors allows you to start before the soil has warmed. They should be well hardened off before planting out.

Buying in plants

Some very nasty pests (such as potato eelworm) can unwittingly be brought into a garden in the soil around the roots of seedlings and plants. Many pests are too small to be seen with the naked eye, so the only way to be sure that this does not happen is to obtain all plants and seedlings from a reputable source, or to raise everything yourself. The latter option is fine for vegetables (apart from potatoes), but propagating fruit plants from your own stock is not advisable unless you are certain that they are one hundred per cent healthy.

The right site

Plants will only grow strongly if they are planted in a situation they enjoy; in the right sort of soil, with the right amount of sunlight (or shade) and protection from the wind. Unhappy plants are always more prone to problems. Gardens do not always provide ideal sites but do the best you can and check before you plant.

Resistant varieties

If you have a persistent problem the answer may be to grow 'resistant' varieties. Examples of these are given under the appropriate crops, but check the catalogues too, as new ones are being introduced all the time. If a variety is *resistant* to a pest, it does not mean that it is *immune*. However, the effects will be less.

Breaking the cycle

If crops such as brassicas or onions are growing all year round, pests can reach epidemic proportions because a suitable host plant is always available. Break the cycle by clearing up all the plants of one type before more of the same are sown. This can help to solve the problem.

The same principle applies to fruit when planting new stocks. Always remove and destroy any old plants that are suffering from a persistent pest or disease *before* introducing the new.

Winter digging

Some pests pass the winter in the soil. Their numbers can be reduced by turning the ground over in winter to expose them to the cold and to predators such as birds.

Also, netting should be removed from the top of the fruit cage over winter to allow the birds in to do their work.

Companion planting/ intercropping

The idea of growing one plant next to another to keep pests at bay is very attractive. Several books have been written listing 'good companions'. Unfortunately there is little evidence that these actually work. However companion planting carrots and onions is effective as it keeps carrot fly at bay (*see page 32*). Brassicas and beans planted together keep aphids and root fly from the brassicas (*see page 31*). Research trials show that details such as plant numbers, timing, etc., must be right for the 'companionship' effect to work.

Know your problem

Before tackling a problem, it is important to know whether you are dealing with a pest, a disease, a virus, a deficiency in the soil or even some environmental factor. Only then can you decide whether anything needs to be done and if so, what. It is very frustrating and a waste of time and energy trying to deal with the wrong cause.

It is helpful to know the life cycle and habits of a pest in order to devise ways of avoiding or coping with it.

Crop rotation

Crop rotation simply means that the same type of plant is not grown on the same piece of ground every year. Rotation prevents drastic build up of soil-living pests and diseases and makes soil management simpler.

In the vegetable garden, for example, moving the potatoes to a different plot each year will help to reduce the buildup of eelworm – if you are unlucky enough to have this pest. By doing this the eelworms will have nothing to feed on until potatoes are planted in this same plot several years later. Also, because the potato crop is the one that tends to be manured, it means that, over a period of years, the whole vegetable garden is treated. A three or four year rotation is good, but a five or six year cycle (if this is possible) is even better.

An example of a four year rotation is given here, but there are many variations on this theme. Gardeners usually work out the rotation that suits themselves and their vegetables best.

When planning a rotation there are two factors to bear in mind:
1. Keep together the crops that are prone to the same pests and diseases (see box below).
2. Keep together the plants that like the same soil conditions.

Plant groups that are prone to the same pests and diseases:
- Potatoes and tomatoes
- Onions, garlic, leeks, shallots
- Cabbages, Brussels sprouts, cauliflower, kale, sprouting broccoli, calabrese, swede, turnip, kohlrabi, radish, mustard
- Carrots, parsley, parsnips, celery
- Peas and beans of all sorts; winter tares
- Courgettes and pumpkins

In the fruit garden, annual rotation is not practical. The plants would not appreciate the moves! But new stock should always be planted on a new site, as far away as possible from the old one.

An example of a four year rotation

Year 1: potatoes.

Year 2: legumes (peas, beans, etc).

Year 3: brassicas (the cabbage family).

Year 4: root crops, including onions, but excluding any brassica root crops.

YEAR 1
POTATOES
ROOTS
BRASSICAS
LEGUMES
YEAR 2
LEGUMES
POTATOES
ROOTS
BRASSICAS
YEAR 3
BRASSICAS
LEGUMES
POTATOES
ROOTS
YEAR 4
ROOTS
BRASSICAS
LEGUMES
POTATOES

Other crops, such as lettuces, courgettes etc., are fitted in where appropriate, but should still be moved round in rotation.

Protecting your plants

Netting

Flying pests from pigeons and blackbirds to flea beetles and greenfly can be kept at bay with netting. Just choose the mesh size of the net to suit the pest.

Ordinary plastic garden netting is most useful for keeping out cats, dogs, birds, and other large pests. A smaller mesh netting with mesh of 1 cm square or less can be used to protect brassicas from the cabbage white butterflies.

Very small pests such as flea beetles and root flies can be kept out using the fine mesh nets or lightweight spun polyester materials that are now available. Some are used over a framework, (cloche hoops are ideal), but others are so light and soft that they can be laid directly on top of the plants. These porous materials have the advantage over plastic covers in that they let air and water through, so only need to be removed for weeding.

Important: Cover plants *before* the pests arrive. Plants can either remain covered throughout their life, or just while they are particularly vulnerable.

Plastic garden netting.

Fine mesh nets or spun polyester materials make excellent protective coverings for plants.

Commercial 'humming line' to keep off birds (see page 21).

Root fly barriers

Plants of the cabbage family can be protected from the cabbage root fly by placing a 13 cm square of rubbery carpet underlay on the soil

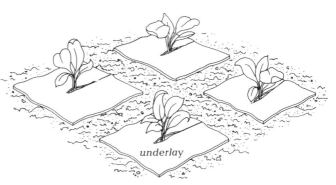

underlay

around the stem at planting time. A barrier of a different type can be used to exclude the carrot root fly.

Fencing

A good fence is really the only effective method of keeping rabbits out of a garden. It should be made of a material with a mesh size of 5 cm or less. To prevent the creatures burrowing underneath, wire netting should be buried in the ground as illustrated.

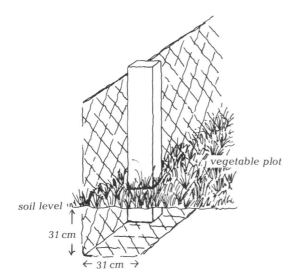

vegetable plot

soil level

31 cm

← 31 cm →

Electric fencing against rabbits is now also possible. It is movable, and avoids the hard work of erecting a conventional fence, but the initial expense will be greater.

A sturdy barrier, 75 cm high, made of polythene or very fine netting, will keep carrot root fly at bay. A size of around 90 cm by 3 m works well. Put it up before, or immediately after sowing.

Bottle cloches

Individual cloches can be made by·cutting off the bottom of a plastic drinks bottle. These cloches afford protection against many pests including slugs – as long as you don't trap one inside! They also keep off cold winds and create a warmer atmosphere for the plants.

Traps

A variety of home-made and commercially available traps can be used to reduce pest numbers. They are unlikely to achieve a long-term reduction, but may help protect crops in the short-term.

Leaf weevils, which can congregate in hordes on raspberries, are easily caught on greased boards held under the canes while the foliage is shaken. Use a heavy grease (like car grease) or one of the non-drying sticky glues that are readily available. Similar boards can be used to catch flea beetles, which jump up when plants are disturbed.

Codling moths can be caught in a sticky trap, to which they are lured by a synthetic 'sex attractant' (pheromone) available from gardening suppliers. The wingless winter moth females can be stopped on their journey up the trunk of a fruit tree by a sticky grease band, (*see page 38*).

The preparation used for this purpose is a special vegetable grease. Ordinary car grease should not be used.

In the vegetable plot, home-made traps can be used for slugs, wireworms and millipedes.

A synthetic sex hormone lures male codling moths to a sticky end in this trap.

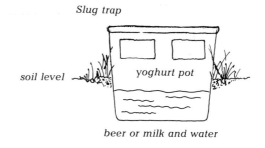

Slug trap

soil level   *yoghurt pot*

beer or milk and water

Hand picking

Nip problems in the bud by picking off infected shoots and leaves at an early stage. Summer pruning of soft fruit bushes has a similar effect. Larger pests such as caterpillars and slugs are easily removed by hand.

General fruit and vegetable pests

This chapter should be used with the identification charts at the back of this book, see pages 40–43.

The pests described here are not particularly fussy in their choice of food and therefore can be a problem to a wide range of totally unrelated plants

Aphids   Fruit and vegetables

These small, soft-bodied insects come in a range of colours, but are often lumped together under the same name 'greenfly' or 'blackfly'. Some types of aphid will attack only a single, or a small number of species of plant. Others have wider tastes. The one pictured above on this page is the potato aphid, the one below is a lettuce leaf aphid.

Aphids tend to live in fast-growing colonies. They feed on plant sap and this activity weakens and distorts growth. They secrete a sticky 'honeydew', which falls on to leaves and pods on which black sooty moulds grow. Sooty moulds are not in themselves harmful, but they prevent light getting to the leaves, cause premature leaf fall, and spoil the appearance. Some species protect themselves by making leaves pucker and curl, or by living under a woolly coating which makes control difficult. Aphids can also transmit viral diseases.

Aphids overwinter both as eggs and sometimes as adults. In the spring winged youngsters fly off to infest lush, young plants. They breed quickly, producing live, wingless offspring. When the plants begin to mature, winged aphids are again produced and these fly off to new host plants. Some will remain there for the winter, while others will fly off to overwinter on a plant unrelated to the summer host.

Prevention
Plants with correct growing conditions and a balanced food supply are much less attractive to aphids.

Their natural enemies are legion: including hover-flies, ladybirds, parasitic wasps, anthocorids, spiders, earwigs and birds. The section 'Know and encourage your friends' beginning on page 4 describes ways to encourage these creatures in the garden. Remember that many of these beneficial creatures need aphids to feed and breed on, so where aphids are not causing any real problem, leave them as reserve food supplies, to keep your 'friends' happy.

Once infested
Infested leaves, shoots etc., can be picked off, or the aphids knocked off with a strong jet of water.

Note: some more specific methods of dealing with aphids are listed in the 'Crop by crop' section.

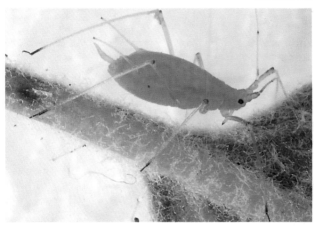

Actual size ×13

Actual size ×14

Birds

Fruit and vegetables

Birds account for enormous numbers of pests, but unfortunately they themselves can also be pests. Fruit, in particular, is a great favourite of several common birds, especially the jay pictured above, and bullfinch damage to winter buds of fruit bushes and trees can be severe. Pigeons are a problem for vegetables, destroying a cabbage patch in no time at all.

Prevention

Marauding birds soon get used to most scaring devices, so to be at all effective these devices should be changed every week or so.

Winter bullfinch damage may be reduced by providing alternative food sources, e.g. seed heads of teasel etc., which the finches prefer.

Netting susceptible crops is the only really effective method of preventing attack. Where the risk is less, scaring techniques, can be tried, such as:

● Video, computer or cassette tape, stretched between canes. This will flash in the light and make a noise in the wind.

● Commercial 'humming line', which also makes a noise in the wind *(see page 18)*.

● Pieces of hosepipe laid out to look like snakes.

● Children's plastic windmills and anything else that flaps, turns or makes a noise in the wind.

Capsid bugs

Mainly fruit

There are a number of species of this small shield-shaped winged bug, some specific to certain host plants such as the potato capsid and apple capsid, but the common green capsid has widespread tastes. All bush or tree fruits are potential food sources for capsids. They feed on leaves, buds and flowers leaving irregular ragged holes in leaves whilst flowers, buds and fruits are distorted. Apples show raised bumps and irregularities in shape but are perfectly edible and can be stored.

Capsids feed at night, move fast and are very hard to catch. Fortunately plants can usually

Actual size ×6

tolerate their damage, so long as virus is not transmitted through injection of saliva, in which case there is no effective method of control.

Cats and dogs

Remember your much loved pets can create havoc in the garden. Cats can be excluded from seed drills or sensitive seedlings with low netting or pea sticks. It is advisable to train your dog not to go on the garden.

Cutworms   Vegetables

Cutworms are large, squashy, soil-living caterpillars. They vary in colour but all curl up like a 'C' when disturbed. They feed at night on the soil surface, eating off young plants at ground level. They often work along a row, leaving wilting and dead specimens in their wake. Cutworms also feed on stems, roots and tubers of crops such as celery, beetroot, carrots, potatoes and strawberries.

22

These pests are the caterpillars of various moth species, which lay their eggs on plants, and plant debris in June/July. The caterpillars feed for a couple of months before they are ready to become moths. These moths again lay eggs and the resulting caterpillars overwinter in the soil, feeding whenever the weather is warm enough. They pupate in the spring.

Actual size ×4

Prevention
Where cutworms have been a problem, winter digging may reduce their numbers. Blackbirds love them. The most efficient answer, if you have them, is to let a flock of hens run over the plot — when it is fallow of course!

Individual plants can be protected with collars of tin or plastic drainpipe, pressed down a few centimetres into the soil.

Once infested
During the growing season, individuals may be picked up by hand, from just under the soil surface in daytime, or on it at night. Regular hoeing helps to disturb them.

Earwigs   Fruit
Forficula auricularia

These brown insects, with prominent pincers at one end, have a worse reputation than they deserve (*see picture on page 8*). They are powerful predators and eat a considerable number of insect eggs, including those of the codling moth. They are only a minor pest of fruit trees, although they do damage some fruit, especially apples. They are often found hiding round apple stalks, but generally only use cavities on fruits, or other damage already created by birds and wasps, for concealment rather than feeding. Damage to flowers and leaves is likely to be slight.

Damaged apples have small, slightly discoloured soft patches, punctured by tiny black feeding holes. Such fruit is edible but will not store.

Since earwigs are more of a friend than an enemy, try not to kill them. This is a diffcult task anyway.

Leather-jackets   Vegetables
Tipula spp. and *Nephrotoma*

This soil-living pest is the larva of the familiar gangly 'daddy-long-legs' or crane-fly. The larvae are a dull, grey-brown colour and are mainly a pest of lawns in autumn, spring and summer. They also feed, however, on the roots of some vegetable crops; brassicas in particular. Normally they are only a problem on soils recently prepared from old lawns or pastures or on particularly weedy plots. Sometimes they may persist for a few years after initial cultivation, but damage should decrease gradually.

Actual size ×4

There are no suitable sprays or soil treatments for this pest. Regular cultivation and the maintenance of a weed-free plot should reduce damage.

Mice and Voles   Vegetables and fruit

Field mice can cause havoc in early spring and autumn sowings of peas and beans. Voles are very partial to beetroot and carrots and will also nibble Jerusalem artichokes and potatoes, especially those grown on a no-dig system. Voles also cause damage to roots of fruit bushes and trees.

Prevention

Conventional traps can be set outdoors, preferably under some form of cover so that other animals and birds are not caught. An alternative is to use 'humane' traps, which catch mice alive.

If mice are a real problem, keeping a cat may be a good deterrent.

If seeds of peas and beans are being eaten, it may help to delay sowing until early summer when more food is around for the mice. Well-grown transplants are less likely to be eaten. Beans can be raised in home–made paper pots; rows of peas in lengths of plastic guttering. These can be suspended above the ground if mice attack them too!

If mice and voles are seriously damaging tree roots, it is advisable to apply no surface mulch.

Millipedes   Vegetables

Millipedes are slim, many legged, segmented creatures, up to 6 cm long. They move quite slowly and smoothly, coiling up like a spring when at rest. They have two pairs of legs per segment (unlike the fast moving centipedes which have one pair per segment, (*see page 10*) and can be one of several colours including shiny black, yellow with red spots, and brown and white.

Actual size ×2

Millipedes feed mainly on dead plant material such as leaf litter and wood, but they will also eat young seedlings. They will extend wounds in tubers and roots made by other creatures but are not able to initiate this sort of damage. You will always find the damage below ground level but it is not easily recognizable as being caused by millipedes. The only way to be sure is to look in the surrounding soil for the pest.

Millipedes live and breed in the soil, especially in undisturbed accumulations of plant debris. They prefer moist soil, rich in organic matter. They are not an easy pest to control.

Prevention
On a small scale, millipedes *may* be distracted from seedlings with a millipede trap. A trap can be made with a piece of cut potato or carrot skewered on a stick, or stuffed into perforated tin cans and buried in the soil. These should be replaced regularly and any trapped millipedes disposed of.

Digging the soil will disturb them and expose them to attack by their enemies which include birds, hedgehogs, frogs, toads and ground beetles.

Rabbits

Rabbits can consume a whole crop in one night if present in numbers, (*see the chapter on 'Protecting your plants', on page 17*).

Slugs and snails   Fruit and vegetables

Four species of slug are common garden pests. They range in colour from pinky/fawn to black and reach up to 10 cm in length. They feed on a wide range of plants. Seedlings may be eaten off as they come up, larger plants reduced to shreds, and fruit, roots and tubers eaten to hollow shells. Often a tell tale slime trail identifies the culprit.

Slugs lose water rapidly in dry weather and they dislike light, so feeding tends to be by night and on dull days after rain. Damage is always worse in warm wet weather.

In autumn, some species will move down into the soil as the temperature drops; others can keep feeding at very low temperatures 1–2°C (33–35°F).

Slug eggs are transparent or opaque little globules, found in cavities in the soil and are laid at almost any time of year.

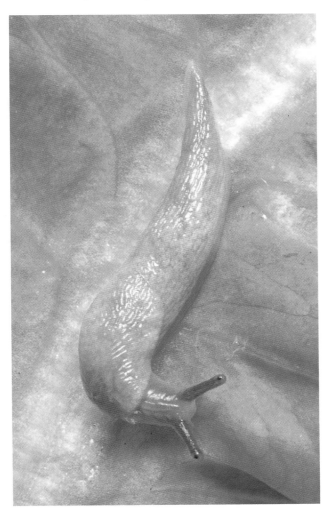

Coping with slugs

There is no simple, single method of coping with slugs organically. The ideas included in the following list have all worked for someone at some time; a combination of several is more likely to succeed.

● Encourage quick seedling germination and growth. (*see page 14*)

● Transplant from modules or pots rather than bare root; harden off well.

● Cover plants with plastic bottle cloches (but don't trap a slug inside).

● Surround plants with a wide barrier of dry materials such as sawdust, bark, woodash or soot. Rain will soon reduce their effectiveness, but cloches may help.

● Lay out old lettuce leaves between young seedlings as an alternative food supply. Slugs prefer dead and dying plants and will be attracted to them to feed. The slugs can then be picked off at night. If the leaves are covered with something to keep them moist, such as a roof tile, or piece of wood, they will last longer, and the slugs feeding on them can be picked up during the day.

● Handpicking and trapping are unlikely to have any long-term effect on slug numbers but can give protection at vulnerable stages. Pick slugs off plants at night (by torchlight). Many will collect under wet cardboard or newspaper and can then be collected and dropped into salty water, or squashed etc.

● Traps, consisting of a yoghurt pot half buried in the soil and filled with beer or milk, may catch large numbers (*see page 19*). Alter the bait now and again, and stop using traps if they catch ground beetles as they eat slugs.

● Where potato slugs are a problem, harvest the crop by early September as this is the month in which most damage is caused.

● An autumn-dug soil, left rough, helps slugs survive a bad winter by allowing them to go far down into the soil to hibernate. If you must dig, do it in the cold of winter for maximum distruption of eggs and slugs.

● If you keep a flock of hens on the land, or some ducks, they will make short work of the slugs. If you can't keep such livestock, try to encourage other slug enemies — hedgehogs, frogs, toads, ground beetles, and slow-worms.

● As a last resort see page 46.

Swift moth caterpillars
Hepialus spp.

Fruit and vegetables

Swift moth caterpillars are white with a shiny brown head and they can be up to 6.5 cm in length. They live in the soil and feed on roots and tubers. They also eat into the stems of plants.

The moths lay eggs from June to August, in weedy ground for preference. The caterpillars are a common sight when ground is being cleared. They feed through the winter and may continue for another year before maturing into adults.

Actual size ×4

Prevention
Regular weed control will limit egg laying, and winter digging may reduce numbers in the soil. If weedy land being brought into cultivation is seen to contain this pest, it should be thoroughly cleared and cultivated before planting up.

Wasps
Paravespula spp.

Fruit

Wasps are so familiar that they need no description. Fertile queens build small papery nests in the spring to start a nuclear brood which, when hatched, continue to expand the nest rapidly, building large colonies under suitable conditions. Surprisingly much of their diet consists of caterpillars, aphids and insects and it is only in high summer and autumn that they become a major pest of all fruit, sometimes stripping a plum to leave nothing but a dry stone hanging from the tree. In dry hot summers damage will be worse because of increased numbers.

Prevention
Jam jars part filled with sugary water, or jam and water, and suspended in trees will catch many wasps. Derris dust can be used, see page 46.

Weevils, leaf

Fruit and vegetables

Ceutorhynchus spp., *Phyllobius* spp.

Weevils are a type of beetle, easily distinguished by their pointed snouts. They feed on leaves of a number of different plant groups, including peas, beans, brassicas and some fruit. Leaf weevils of fruit (*Phyllobius* spp.) have a metallic bronze or green sheen and feed on leaves of raspberries, pears and other tree fruits in May and June. Damage is seldom severe but an infestation can temporarily check plant growth.

Actual size ×13

Prevention and once infested

A greased board held under a branch where weevils are feeding will catch hundreds at a time if the branch is shaken.

Wireworms

Strawberries and vegetables

Agriotes spp.

Wireworms are slender, yellowy-brown, beetle larvae with tough shiny skins; they have three pairs of legs at the head end of the body. They can grow up to 2.5 cm in length.

Wireworm feed on the underground parts (stems, tubers, roots) of many vegetables, including lettuce, onions, tomatoes, potatoes, beetroot, carrots, peas, beans and strawberries. The amount of damage depends on the stage of growth and vigour of the plants. Seedlings wilt and die; older plants may survive, possibly with reduced vigour. Lettuce and tomatoes are at risk at a later stage because the wireworm tunnels up into the stem. Mature potato tubers and carrot roots are also attacked, the initial small hole often being enlarged by other pests.

Wireworm are the larvae of the click beetle which lay its eggs in summer, mainly in grassland or weedy soil. The resulting larvae feed for up to five years, the main feeding period being from March to May. They also feed, less actively, in September and October.

Because they do not like being disturbed, wireworm can often be found in large numbers in pasture and rough land.

Actual size ×2

Prevention

If old grass or pasture land is being brought into cultivation, the best time is February and March. Wireworms will be feeding in the turf, and if this is buried deeply the wireworm should stay down with it, feeding for a couple of years before coming up to cause damage. If land is kept weed-free, the wireworms should have flown after five years, with no new ones to replace them.

Sometimes wireworms remain a problem even on cultivated land. Various strategies can be used to help reduce the damage:

● Encourage quick germination and growth of seedlings, (*see page 14*).

● Sow into a firm seedbed and delay thinning as long as possible.

● Cultivate the land, to expose them to the birds that eat them.

● In small areas wireworm can be caught in pieces of potato or carrot spiked on sticks and buried in the ground. These should be replaced regularly.

● Peas and beans are less attractive to wireworm than other crops.

● Harvest potatoes by early September, to limit autumn feeding damage.

Vegetable pests, crop by crop

This chapter should be used with the identification charts at the back of this book, see pages 40–43.

Asparagus

Asparagus beetle *Crioceris asparagi*
These distinctive chequered beetles and their plump grey/black larvae are the main pest of asparagus, feeding on the foliage and stems from May onwards. Persistent attacks may check growth.

Prevention

Actual size ×7

● In the autumn, clear up accumulated plant debris from the bed, as this is where many beetles will spend the winter.

Once infested
● As a last resort, see page 46.

Beans
Broad, French, runner

Bean seed fly *Delia platura*
Small white maggots feed on germinating pea and bean seeds early in the season. Seedlings die or fail to appear. Worst in cold springs when growth is slow.

Bean seed flies emerge from the soil in late spring and lay their eggs in soil or on seedlings.

Prevention
● Encourage quick early growth, (*see page 14*), or use transplants.

● Fork the soil over two weeks before sowing.
● Sow under a protective cover, (*see page 17*).

Once infested
● There is no cure.

Actual size ×9

Bean weevil (*see picture above and 'Pea and bean weevil', page 34.***)**

Blackfly Black bean aphid *Aphis fabae*
Black 'greenfly' form colonies on the growing tips; they may then spread to the rest of the plant,

28

including pods. A severe infestation can stunt growth and reduce the crop.

Blackfly overwinter as eggs on spindle bushes and appear first on the tips of broad beans in May. As the plants mature the blackfly move on to other beans (French and runner), beetroot, leaf beet and chard, and ornamentals such as nasturtiums, poppies and dahlias. The blackfly that infest elder trees are a different species.

Prevention

● Sow broad beans in the autumn, so that the plants are tougher and less attractive in the spring.

Once infested

● Pick out infested tips of broad beans.

For more information see 'aphids' on page 20

Blossom or pollen beetle *Meligethes aeneus*
Small, shiny black beetles appear in large numbers around June/July, having just left the flowering oilseed rape crops. The beetles can be found on and in a wide range of flowers, including runner beans. They are often blamed for poor runner bean crops but, although they do eat pollen, they do not prevent pod set and no control measures are necessary. Poor cropping is generally a result of hot, dry soil and air conditions.

One crop that pollen beetles can harm is calabrese; they graze the calabrese heads, making them unattractive to eat.

Prevention

● Calabrese crops can be protected by covering the plants with a fine, lightweight material (*see page 17*), before the pests arrive.

Once infested

● There are no good measures to take once the beetles have infested a plant.

Beetroot and spinach beet

Black bean aphid (*see 'Blackfly' page 28.***)**

Leaf miner *Pegomya hyoscyami*
Leaves show blotchy brown 'blisters', made by the leaf miner grub. This can check growth on young plants; it is not really a problem on older beetroot, but it looks unpleasant on leaf beet and tends to be worse in cool weather.

Eggs are laid under leaves in spring; the larvae eat into the leaves to feed for a few weeks then return to the soil to pupate. There are two or three generations a year.

Prevention

● Winter dig where this pest was a problem.
● Encourage quick early growth (*see page 14*). Grow plants under a protective cover, (*see page 17*).

Once infested

● Squash larvae within the leaves.
● Pick off infested leaves.

Brassicas

including broccoli, Brussels sprouts, cabbage, Chinese cabbage, calabrese, kale, kohlrabi, radish, swede and turnip.

Mealy cabbage aphid *Brevicoryne brassicae*
This 'floury' grey aphid forms large colonies on leaves which become distorted and discoloured. A severe attack can kill young plants, or prevent them from cropping. Older plants are less troubled.

Mealy aphids are present all the year round, spending the winter as adults or eggs on winter brassicas and move to new young plants in the spring.

Prevention

● Break the cycle: bury all winter brassica stumps, as soon as cropping has finished, in the compost heap or compost trench. Do this *before* any new susceptible plants are put out.

Once infested

● Check plants regularly, especially newly planted seedlings, from June on. Squash the aphids, or see page 20.

Caterpillars, large white *Pieris brassicae*
(Caterpillars illustrated top right, eggs second right, butterfly third right.)

These are impressive yellow and black caterpillars which feed on leaves and they vary in size enormously. The leaves of young plants may be stripped completely, and those of older plants reduced to holes and tatters. Eggs are laid in groups on the undersides of leaves in April/May, July/Aug and in September in some regions. Note the beautiful symmetry of the eggs.

Caterpillars, small white *Pieris rapae*
(Caterpillar illustrated bottom right)

These caterpillars are smaller, solitary, and velvety green. Eggs are laid singly in March/April, June/July and, the peak laying season, August/September. Damage as for large white.

Caterpillars, Cabbage moth *Mamestra brassicae*
(Not illustrated)

These are large plump caterpillars ranging from light green to brown. They feed on leaves and bore into the hearts of cabbages and cauliflowers. There is only one generation a year, with eggs laid in May/June.

Prevention

● Grow under netting with a mesh of 1 cm square or less (*see page 17*).

Once infested

● Squash eggs and pick off caterpillars. As a last resort, see page 46.

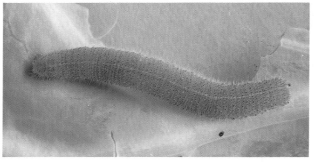

Cabbage root fly *Delia radicum*
(Not illustrated)

Stunted and wilting brassica plants are usually the first sign of this pest. The plants are easily pulled up because the small white root fly larvae have eaten away the roots. Older plants can survive an attack, though in the case of root crops (radish, turnip, swede) they can be rendered inedible.

Root flies overwinter as small brown shiny cocoons in the soil. Adults hatch when cow parsley comes into flower (early May), and lay their eggs in the soil around brassica plants. The second generation (July/August) is the most troublesome in oilseed rape growing areas; there may also be a third.

Prevention
- Winter dig the soil after an infected crop.
- Rotation.
- Break the cycle, (*see cabbage whitefly opposite*).
- Grow under a protective cover, (*see page 17*).
- Put 12 cm square mats of rubbery carpet underlay around young transplants.
- Intercrop with beans, (*see box below*).
- Raise transplants in 7–8 cm, or bigger pots, so that they have a good root system when planted out.

Once infested
- Earth up stems to encourage new root growth.

Intercropping for cabbage pest control
Intercropping plants of the cabbage family with other, unrelated, plants will reduce the damage caused by both cabbage root fly and mealy aphids. It seems that the mixture misleads and confuses the pests, so fewer root fly eggs are laid, and fewer aphids colonize the brassicas. The increased ground cover intercropping gives also encourages natural predators, such as ground beetles.

Research shows that dwarf broad and French beans are both good for intercropping. Grow brassicas and beans in alternate rows 25 cm apart. The outer rows must be beans. For a good crop from both beans and brassicas, the plants need to be about the same size when planted out. If you want a mixture of summer cabbage and French beans, sow the cabbage about three weeks before the beans. Plant out when a reasonable size. French beans should at least have their first pair of leaves fully grown. If they do not, the diversionary tactics of the mixture do not work immediately which is just when the brassica plants are at their most vulnerable.

Brassica whitefly *Aleyrodes proletella*
This is a common pest which usually looks much worse than it is! Tiny white flies live on the undersides of leaves and fly up in a cloud when disturbed. They may make leaves sticky with honeydew, which turns into harmless sooty moulds.

Whitefly can be found on brassicas all year round. They stop breeding in the winter but can still be active.

Actual size × 30

Prevention
- Break the cycle. Remove all overwintered brassicas in the early spring, before new plants are transplanted. Bury all old plants in the compost heap, or in a compost trench.

Once infested
- Pick off lower leaves infested with whitefly larvae. As a last resort see page 46.

Flea beetles *Phyllotreta* spp.
These small dark shiny beetles are a pest of brassicas and other related crucifers, eating small holes in leaves of seedlings and also of larger plants of the more tender brassicas such as Chinese cabbage. Losses can be severe, especially in hot dry seasons.

Actual size × 9

Flea beetles hibernate in plant debris, and under loose bark on trees. They first appear in April or May (when midday temperatures reach 20°C (68°F)). Eggs are laid in the soil and new adults start to feed in August.

Prevention
● Encourage quick early growth, (*see page 14*).
● Sow/transplant under a protective cover (*see page 17*).
● Ensure seedlings and young plants are never short of water.

Once infested
● Use a sticky board, (*see page 19*), to trap the beetles which jump up as plants are disturbed. As a last resort see page 46.

Blossom/pollen beetles
See Bean section on page 29.

Carrots

Carrot root fly *Psila rosae*
Carrot root fly larvae feed on roots of carrot, celery, celeriac, parsnip, parsley and chervil. Seedlings may be killed; older plants may show a reddening of the leaves and growth may be stunted. Roots will have 'rusty' coloured galleries tunnelled in them and small white larvae may be present. If damage is severe carrot roots may be inedible.

Carrot root fly overwinter in the soil, and in roots left in the ground, emerging in May/June to lay eggs in the soil near suitable crops; the larvae feed for a month then pupate in the soil. A second generation of adults will emerge in Aug/Sept.

Actual size × 13

Prevention
● Rotation.
● Sow carrots in Feb/ early March or delay till June.
● Grow on a windy site.
● Dig over land that has been infected to let the birds at the pupae.
● Intercrop four rows of onions between each row of carrots. This protective effect lasts only until the onion leaves stop growing. They stop when the bulbs start to form.
● Grow under a protective cover, (*see page 17*), or within a carrot fly barrier, (*see picture on page 18*).

Once infested
● Carrots and parsnips for use during the winter should be lifted in the autumn and stored in a shed. Left in the ground, carrot root fly damage will continue and get worse.

Celery

Celery fly/leaf miner *Euleia heracleii*
Larvae tunnel within leaves of celery, celeriac and parsnip, causing blotchy brown 'mines' which later dry up to give a scorched look. A bad attack can stunt growth and make celery tough.

Celery flies emerge from the soil in spring to lay eggs on suitable leaves. The larvae feed for a month then pupate in leaf or soil. There are up to three generations a year, so this pest can be a problem all season.

Prevention
● Grow plants under a protective cover, (*see page 17*).

Once infested
● Pick off infested leaves, or squash the larvae within them to reduce future generations.

Lettuce

Lettuce root aphid *Pemphigus bursarius*
Infected plants will be stunted and may wilt suddenly. A closer look will reveal white 'floury' aphids on the roots.

This aphid usually spends the winter on poplar trees, moving on to lettuces in June, but some may remain in the soil over winter.

Prevention
● Grow resistant varieties, e.g. Avoncrisp, Avondefiance.
● Rotation.
● Winter digging.

Once infested
● Remove infested plants, to reduce spread.

Lettuce leaf aphids *various*
Three sorts of aphids can infect lettuce leaves. A

heavy attack can make the crop unpalatable and stunt growth. Check young plants regularly and deal with the problem as shown on page 20.

Onions and related crops
including, spring onions, garlic, leeks, shallots, and chives.

Onion fly *Delia antiqua*
These flies attack onions, shallots and leeks. The fly larvae (white maggots, up to 1 cm in length) feed on roots, killing young plants and damaging bulbs which then rot.

Adults look like small house-flies and emerge from the soil in May, to lay their eggs on, or near, suitable plants. The larvae hatch out and feed for three weeks, then return to the soil to pupate. There may be two or three generations a year, but the first is the worst.

Prevention
● Rotation.
● Winter dig infected land.
● Grow under a protective cover, (*see page 17*).

Once infested
● Remove infested plants to reduce spread.

Stem eelworm *Ditylenchus dipsaci*
This microscopic pest can attack a wide range of plants - fruit, ornamentals, weeds and vegetables. On onions the leaves swell and distort, bulbs crack and rot. Plants will crop badly, and may die. Similar symptoms occur on leeks and garlic.

Once the plants begin to rot, this eelworm moves back into the soil where it can survive for a considerable time even in the absence of a host.

Prevention
● Rotation.
● Grow only brassicas and/or lettuce (which this eelworm does not attack) on the infested plot for the next two years, and keep it weed-free. It should then be safe to return to onion growing.

Once infested
● There is no cure for infested plants, which should be dug up and disposed of outside the garden.

Parsnips

Carrot root fly (*see page 32*)

Peas

Pea moth *Cydia nigricana*

Pea moth caterpillars live and feed inside pea pods. They may damage only one or two peas, or make their way through the whole pod. They can devastate a crop grown for the production of dried peas. The moth lays its eggs in June and July on pea plants that are in flower. The tiny caterpillars quickly eat their way into developing pods, feed for a month and then return to the soil to pupate. There is only one generation a year.

Prevention

● Sow peas early and late (eg. February and May), so they are not in flower in June/July.

● Winter dig infested plots.

● Cover peas with a very fine mesh netting while they are in flower especially in early July. As a last resort, see page 46.

Once infested

● There is no cure.

Pea thrips *Kakothrips robustus*

Thrips, commonly known as thunderflies, attack many crops. Those on peas and broad beans are up to 1.7 mm long and a yellow-brown colour; the larvae are yellow. They feed on leaves and pods causing the characteristic silver sheen. Pods may be distorted. Damage can be serious in hot dry weather.

Thrips overwinter in the soil. Adults emerge in late spring to lay their eggs on flower stamens. The larvae feed for two to three weeks then return to the soil. There is one generation a year at its peak from mid-June to end-July.

Prevention

● Winter dig infested plots.

● Water plants regularly in dry spells to keep them cool and moist.

● Misting with water can help.

● Rotation; if attacks are very severe it could be worth not growing peas at all for a couple of years.

Once infested

● If the attack is very severe, see page 46.

Pea and bean weevil *Sitona lineatus*

Small 6 mm grey/brown weevils chew a scalloped edge on leaves of peas, broad beans, clovers and vetches. If plants are growing strongly they are not a problem, but a severe attack on young plants can be serious.

Weevils overwinter in plant debris, moving out in the early spring to lay eggs in the soil. The larvae feed on root nodules, then emerge as adults in June and July. There is one generation a year.

Prevention

● Encourage strong fast growth.

Once infested

● As a last resort, see page 46.

Potatoes

Cyst eelworm (potato sickness) *Globodera* spp.

This microscopic pest feeds on potato roots, stunting growth and reducing crops. Effects can be severe. If you examine the roots at the end of June/ early July you may see small brown or white pinhead cysts. These fall back into the soil where they can survive for at least ten years.

Prevention

● Buy only certified seed tubers.

Once infested

● It is impossible to eliminate eelworm from the soil, but there are various strategies that can help produce some form of crop in infested soil:

● Use as long a rotation as possible.

● Grow early varieties, which do most of their growing before the eelworm attacks.

● Increase levels of organic matter in soil.

● Use the no-dig method of growing under a straw/hay mulch.

● Resistant varieties are of limited use as they are only resistant to one type of cyst eelworm.

Fruit pests, crop by crop

This chapter should be used with the identification charts at the back of this book, see pages 40–43.

Blackberries, raspberries and hybrid berries

Raspberry beetle *Byturus tomentosus*

Adults are found feeding on blossoms in May but it is the larvae that do the most damage. These tunnel into ripening fruit, occasionally causing distortion, but often not noticed until the fruit is picked. Larvae are small (up to 8 mm) and dun-coloured with brown heads and brown side markings. They overwinter in soil near canes.

Actual size ×6

Prevention

● If larvae are noticed during picking, lightly cultivate soil near canes during autumn/winter to expose pupae to birds.

Once infested

● Spray as a last resort, (*see page 46*).

Cane midge *Resseliella theobaldi*

Tiny orange/red larvae no more than 4 mm long feed in cracks in the bark of new canes. Immediate damage is light but cane blight often invades damaged areas causing canes to die back. Adults emerge from soil in May or June and lay eggs in wounds and crevices on canes. Larvae feed for a month before pupating in soil. This cycle may be repeated three times or more between July and the end of summer.

Prevention

● Lightly cultivate soil around base of canes during winter to expose pupae to birds.

Once infested

● Only spray as a last resort, (*see page 46*).

Froghoppers *Philaenus spumarius*

Most gardeners will be familiar with the white frothy blobs of 'cuckoo spit' that appear first in May. Inside each of these blobs is a nymph of the froghopper, aptly named for its shape and habit of jumping when disturbed. Generally cuckoo spit is found on ornamental plants, but raspberries and blackberries are frequently affected. The damage to the plant is minimal, despite the alarming appearance of numerous white blobs. If you are keen to get rid of them, a flick of the finger or jet of water will dislodge them.

Blackcurrants

Gall mite (big bud) *Cecidophyopsis ribis*

Mites breed inside developing buds causing them to become characteristically round and swollen, hence the term 'big bud'. Mites carry reversion virus, which is altogether more serious and will cause slow deterioration of the bush and poor cropping.

The mites overwinter in swollen buds, dispersing as these open in March and April to enter young developing buds between then and the end of June. They are sometimes carried in on the wind, by aphids and on birds' feet.

Prevention

● For new plantings buy in good quality bushes from a reputable source.

- Never plant new bushes near infested stock.
- Prevention is impossible on established bushes.

Once infested
- Remove and burn all swollen buds before spring. In severe cases cut back all growth to ground level and burn. As blackcurrants fruit on last year's wood, this will, of course, mean no crop in the following season, but the sacrifice is justified if the pest is controlled.

Leaf midge *Dasineura tetensi*
Tiny orange or white larvae infest top-most leaves on terminal shoots causing leaves to twist, distort and become speckled. Terminal shoots occasionally die and growth can be reduced.

Midges emerge from cocoons in the soil early in spring and lay eggs on unopened leaves at tips of shoots. Larvae hatch a week later, feed for a month and drop to the soil to pupate. This cycle is repeated three or four times until August or September.

Prevention
- Variety Ben Sarek has some resistance. Other resistant varieties are being developed.
- Encourage anthocorid bugs which prey on midges.

Once infested
- Spray as a last resort, (*see page 46*).

Gooseberries

Gooseberry sawfly *Nematus ribesii*
Sawfly larvae can strip leaves on gooseberries and currants very efficiently if unchecked. The larvae are pale green with black spots and reach a final size of about 2.5 cm. Adult flies hatch from cocoons in the soil in April and lay white eggs on backs of leaves along veins, mainly low in the centre of the bush. Hatching larvae feed and create easily

spotted pin-hole effects on leaves. Mature larvae pupate in the soil. There may be three or four generations each year from late April to early September.

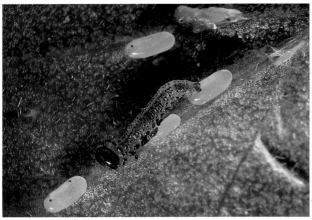

Actual size ×2

Prevention
- None.

Once infested
- Inspect bushes regularly at end of April, early June, late June/early July and early September. Pick off pin-holed leaves and crush eggs.
- Spray as a last resort, (*see page 46*).

Magpie moth *Abraxas grossulariata*
Similar damage to gooseberry sawfly, April to June.

Caterpillars are black, white and yellow 'loopers'.

See 'sawfly' on this page for details of how to deal with this pest.

Strawberries

Red spider mite *Tetranychus urticae*
Normally a pest in greenhouses, this mite can be troublesome on outdoor strawberries (also raspberries and currants) in a hot year. The undersurfaces of the leaves are discoloured and bronzed

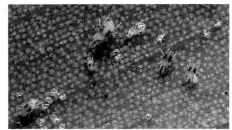

Actual size ×7

and older leaves become brown and withered, or crisp. A magnifying glass will reveal the tiny mites, which, despite their name, are greenish/transparent in colour with two distinct spots. Only the overwintering females are bright orange/red. They breed on leaves during the spring and summer, hibernating in crevices over winter.

Prevention

● Cut off all leaves after fruit is harvested.

● Clear up thoroughly in autumn, removing any mulch and old leaves.

Once infested

● *Phytoseiulus persimilis*, the predatory mite normally used to control mites in the greenhouse, can be used outside in a good summer if introduced in late June or July.

Apples

Codling moth *Cydia pomonella*
A widespread pest, principally of apples, but also affecting pears and quinces. The traditional maggot in the apple. Adults hatch from cocoons in crevices and cracks in June/July to lay eggs on leaves and fruit. Caterpillars tunnel into maturing fruit and feed there for several weeks before pupating, making fruit unsuitable for storing and particularly unappetising. In a hot summer a second generation will hatch in August.

Prevention

● Pheromone traps, which are available to the gardener, will catch many male moths and thus reduce the egg-laying potential of females, see picture on page 19. The traps are hung in a tree from mid-May until the end of July, or early September in a hot dry year.

Once infested

● Traps are insufficient for large populations of moths, or large numbers of trees, but give a good indication of when to spray for best effect. Only spray as a last resort (*see page 46*).

Fruit tree red spider mite *Panonychus ulmi*
These mites affect apples, pears, plums and damsons causing initial speckling and bronzing of leaves and finally drying of leaves which fall prematurely. Mites overwinter as eggs, sometimes visible as small red clusters, and hatch out during April to June. The worst effects are normally seen in June and July but continue until September when the fourth or fifth generation lay eggs to overwinter.

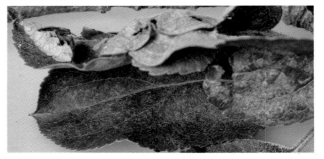

The folded leaves at the top of the picture show tortrix moth damage. The leaves below are infested with spider mite.

Prevention

● Encourage beneficial predators such as Typhlodromid mites and Anthocorid bugs which effectively keep pest numbers down. Avoid frequent use of Derris.

Once infested

● Difficult. Inspect leaves with magnifying glass in May/June. If only a few leaves are affected, pick off and destroy. Use a spray as a last resort (*see page 46*).

Apple sawfly *Hoplocampa testudinea*
Similar damage to the codling moth, but earlier in the season. The cavities in the fruit are filled with 'frass'. Most affected fruitlets drop early, helping the thinning process, but some remain to develop into mature fruit with characteristic ribbon scarring and distortions.

Cocoons in the soil hatch in spring and the adult flies lay eggs in open blossoms in April/May. Eggs hatch two weeks later at about petal fall and the larvae tunnel immediately into fruitlets, feeding on flesh and seeds. Each larvae may visit several fruitlets before dropping to the soil in June or July to form cocoons.

Prevention

● Pick up and compost all fallen fruitlets in June and July.

Once infested

● Use a spray as a last resort, *(see page 46).*

Winter moths
Operophtera brumata, Alsophila aescularia, Erannis defoliaria

Three different moth species are responsible for similar damage to apples, pears, plums and several ornamental plants. In spring buds, blossom and young leaves are eaten by looper caterpillars coloured green, yellow or brown. Leaves become distorted and tattered and blossom fails. If disturbed, caterpillars often drop on a thread to avoid detection. Females are wingless and emerge from the soil between October and April, depending on the species, and climb the trunk or tree stake to lay eggs near buds or in cracks in the bark. March moth eggs are laid on twigs in visible bracelets. Larvae hatch in spring and feed until about June when they drop to the soil on threads to pupate.

Prevention

● Grease bands on trunks *and* tree stakes will catch female moths climbing up the trunk. Have them in place by late October and keep them tacky until the end of April.

Once infested

● Pick off caterpillars by hand.
● Use a spray as a last resort, *(see page 46).*

Tortrix moth
Archips podana, Adoxophyes orana, Pammene rhediella

Another group of moths of distinct species causing similar damage to apples, pears, plums and cherries. It is often not serious. Green caterpillars up to 2.5 cm long feed on buds and leaves and tunnel into fruit during the summer. Leaves are drawn together with threads to protect the feeding site. Female moths lay eggs on leaves in the summer and caterpillars from these feed for a month before pupating. The next generation emerges in autumn and caterpillars born from this generation survive the winter in cocoons and feed on buds and young leaves in the spring.

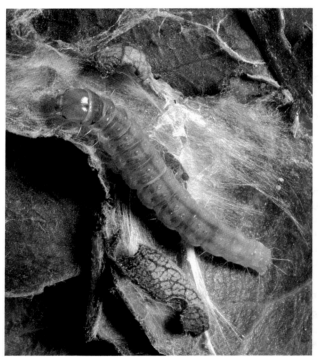

Actual size ×5

Prevention

● None.

Once infested

● Pick off caterpillars, investigating "webbed" leaves carefully. Webbing of leaves makes spraying impractical. Damage is usually not serious.

Cherries

Pear and cherry slugworm
(see 'Pears' on page 39).

Pears

Codling moth (*see 'Apples' on page 37*)

Fruit tree red spider mite
(*see 'Apples' on page 37*).

Leaf blister mites *Eriophyes pyri*
Pink or yellow/green pustules show on leaves in May, turning dark and causing leaf fall later. Tiny mites are feeding within the leaves to cause these blisters.

Adults overwinter in buds and start feeding on leaves in spring. Developing colonies continue to feed through the summer.

Prevention
● None.

Once infested
● Pick off affected leaves early. No other cure available. Damage seldom serious.

Pear midge *Contarinia pyrivora*
Orange-white larvae of this midge feed within the fruitlets causing them to swell, blacken and drop. It can be a serious pest in southern England.

Cocoons in soil over winter give rise to adults in March/April. Females fly into trees and lay eggs in unopened flower buds. The larvae hatch out within the developing fruitlet, for a month or so. After about six weeks they tunnel their way out of the fruitlet, which may already have dropped to the ground. They move into the soil to form cocoons, where they spend the winter.

Prevention
● Pick up and compost all fallen fruitlets during the summer.
● Remove affected fruitlets immediately they are noticed.
● Cultivate soil near affected trees in winter to expose cocoons.

Once infested
● There is no cure.

Pear and cherry slugworm *Caliroa cerasi*
During late spring and summer, the upper surfaces of pear and cherry leaves are grazed to a skeleton by small shiny black larvae resembling slugs which later turn waxy yellow.

Adult flies emerge from cocoons in the soil between May and June and lay eggs on the leaves. Larvae from these feed for a month and then pupate in the soil. The second generation emerges in July/August.

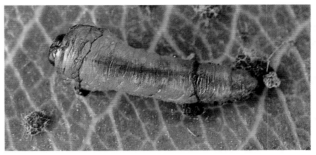

Actual size ×5

Prevention
● If pests have been seen, cultivate soil lightly near affected trees.

Once infested
● Pick off pests.
● Use a spray as a last resort, (*see page 46*).

Winter moth and Tortrix moth
(*see 'Apples' on page 38*).

Plums and damsons

Fruit moth *Cydia funebrana*
These are similar in life cycle and type of damage to Codling moth (*see page 37*). Pinky red maggots feed inside plums and damsons in July/August causing early ripening and falling of fruit.

Prevention
● Pick up and compost all early falling fruit whilst caterpillars are still present.

Once infested
● There is no cure.

Fruit tree red spider mite
(*see 'Apples' on page 37*).

Plum sawfly *Hoplocampa flava*
A cousin of the apple sawfly. Similar damage to the plum fruit moth in spring and early summer, leaving sticky exudate from the entry hole in later stages.

Life cycle is similar to apple sawfly.

Prevention
● Pick up all early fallen fruit as for fruit moth. Damage varies from year to year.

Once infested
● Use a spray as a last resort, as for apple sawfly (*see page 46*).

Tortrix moth and Winter moth
(*see 'Apples' on page 38*).

Identifying vegetable pests at a glance

NAME	SYMPTOM	CAUSE	PAGE
Seedlings, general It is often difficult to know why seedlings fail to emerge, or die once they have done so. Maybe the initial seed was poor, or growing conditions were unsuitable; or they may have been attacked by a number of non-specific pests and diseases. When a problem cannot be identified, the best line of defence is to help them to get a good start, (*see page 14*).	Seedlings fail to appear.	Mice Birds Bean seed fly Millipedes	23 21 28 24
	Seedlings grow poorly or collapse and die. Stems and/or roots chewed.	Cutworm Wireworm Millipedes	22 27 24
	Seedlings with leaves and growing points eaten.	Slugs	25
	Seedlings, especially brassicas, peas and beans, pecked and pulled out of soil.	Birds	21
Asparagus	Leaves and stems eaten. Chequered beetles and/or grey/black larvae may be seen.	Asparagus beetle	28
Beans (French, broad and runner) and peas (*see also 'Seedlings'*)	Semicircular notches eaten out of leaf margins (peas, broad beans).	Pea and bean weevil	34
	Shoots and leaves infested with small black insects; may be sticky.	Blackfly	28
	Leaves and pods with light flecking or silvery sheen (peas, broad beans).	Thrips	34
	Flowers full of small shiny black beetles.	Blossom beetles	29
	Pods with triangular pieces pecked away.	Birds	21
	Pea pods with small, black-headed caterpillars inside; peas eaten.	Pea moth	34
Beetroot and spinach beet (*see also 'Seedlings'*)	Leaves and stems infested with small black insects.	Black bean aphid	29
	Blotchy brown blisters on leaves.	Beet leaf miner	29
	Roots have irregular holes.	Cutworm Swiftmoth	22 26
Brassicas (*see also 'Seedlings'*)	Leaves of seedlings and young plants show pitting and small circular holes.	Flea beetle	31
	Leaves torn, often reduced to a skeleton of veins. Transplants may be pulled out.	Birds	21
	Leaves with irregular holes eaten out.	Caterpillars	30
	Leaves with irregular holes and slime trails.	Slugs	25
	Leaves infested with colonies of floury grey insects; may be discoloured and distorted.	Mealy cabbage aphid	29
	Seedlings and young plants grow poorly and may wilt. Easily pulled up to show roots absent, or being eaten by white maggots.	Cabbage root fly	30
	Leaves, especially underside, infested with small white insects which fly up when disturbed.	Whitefly	31
	Calabrese heads grazed by hordes of tiny black beetles.	Blossom beetles	29

Carrots and parsnips (*see also 'Seedlings'*) The following symptoms can be found on both carrots and parsnips, unless stated.	Carrot leaves with red/yellow mottling; may be twisted; plants stunted.	Carrot root fly	32
	Carrot leaves infested with small green insects.	Carrot willow aphid	20
	Irregular holes in roots; caterpillars in nearby soil.	Cutworm Swift moth caterpillar	22 26
	Roots tunnelled by small white maggots.	Carrot root fly	32
Celery and celeriac (*see also 'Seedlings'*)	Plants collapse; stems eaten off at ground level.	Cutworm	22
	Stems chewed; slime trails visible.	Slugs	25
	Leaves show yellowy-brown blotchy 'mines' which may contain small larvae.	Celery leaf miner	32
	Plants collapse, roots and stem base tunnelled by small maggots.	Carrot root fly	32
Lettuce (*see also 'Seedlings'*)	Seedlings and larger plants unthrifty.	Wireworm Millipedes	27 24
	Plants wilt and die; stem eaten off at ground level.	Cutworm	22
	Plants wilt and die; stem eaten.	Swift moth caterpillar	26
	Leaves infested with small pink or green insects.	Aphids	33
	Plants stunted; may wilt suddenly.	Root aphids	33
Onions, leeks, chives, garlic and shallots, etc.	Seedlings and leaves attacked at or below ground level.	Wireworm Cutworm	27 22
	Leaves wilt, small white maggots in base of bulb.	Onion fly	33
	Base of plant swells early; leaves swollen and distorted.	Stem eelworm	33
Parsley	Leaves with reddish tinge, growth poor; roots tunnelled by small white maggots.	Carrot root fly	32
	Leaves with brown blotchy 'blisters' which may contain larvae.	Celery fly	32
Parsnip (*see also 'Carrots and parsnips'*)	Leaves with yellow–brown blotchy 'mines' which may contain small white larvae.	Celery leaf miner	32
Peas (*see 'Beans and peas'*)			
Potatoes	Leaves yellow, growth poor, crops reduced. Pin-head cysts may be seen on roots.	Potato cyst eelworm	34
	Tubers with holes and galleries which may extend throughout.	Slugs	25
	Tubers with large holes near surface.	Cutworm Swift moth caterpillar	22 26
	Tubers gnawed; tooth marks may be visible.	Mice	23
	Tubers with narrow holes, as if made by a knitting needle.	Wireworm	27
Spinach, annual (*see also 'Seedlings'*)	Leaves with blotchy brown 'blisters' which may have larvae inside.	Leaf miner	29

Identifying fruit pests at a glance

NAME	SYMPTOM	CAUSE	PAGE
Apples	Leaves and shoots infested with small green or pink insects; leaves feel sticky and may be distorted.	Aphids	20
	Leaves and petals chewed; fruit with small 'glassy' patches, punctured with tiny black holes.	Earwigs	22
	Leaves speckled, bronzed or dried up; tiny mites on undersides.	Fruit tree red spider mite	37
	Leaves/shoots with blobs of white froth.	Froghoppers	35
	Young leaves with irregular tattered holes; fruits partly distorted or with raised bumps and discoloured patches.	Capsid bugs	21
	Young leaves tattered in spring; shiny beetles present.	Leaf weevils	27
	Young leaves, flowers and buds eaten; 'loopers' present.	Winter moth	38
	Leaves bound together tightly by threads; caterpillar inside.	Tortrix moth	38
	Fruitlets holed, wet frass in hole, fall prematurely; fruits with ribbon scarring.	Apple sawfly	37
	Fruit with core rotten and tunnelled. Maggot may be present inside.	Codling moth	37
	Fruits with large holes or small pieces chewed or removed.	Birds Wasps	21 26
	Tunnelling under tree; roots damaged.	Voles	23
Blackberries, raspberries and hybrid berries	Underside of leaves infested with small pale green insects; leaves sticky.	Aphids	20
	Dun-coloured larvae feeding in fruits.	Raspberry beetle	35
	Tiny orange/red larvae feeding in cracks in bark of new raspberry canes; tunnelling found in old canes when pruned out.	Cane midge	35
	Leaves with irregular holes	Capsid bugs	21
	Ripe fruits chewed.	Wasps	26
	Leaves/shoots with blobs of white froth.	Froghoppers	35
	Young leaves on fruiting canes chewed by tiny weevils in spring.	Leaf weevils	27
	Leaves speckled, bronzed or dried up; tiny mites on undersides.	Spider mites	37
Blackcurrants	Shoot tips infested with green or yellow insects; leaves curled over and sticky, possibly blistered or distorted.	Aphids	20
	Youngest leaves curled over tightly, speckled and failing to develop.	Leaf midge	36
	Buds swollen and round in winter.	Gall mite	35
	Fruit removed.	Birds	21
	Leaves with irregular holes, especially young leaves.	Capsid bugs	21
Cherries	Tips of shoots infested with black insects; leaves curled over and sticky.	Aphids	20
	Surface of leaves grazed by ...ll, black slug-like larvae.	Pear and cherry slugworm	39
	Buds pecked out in winter; few flowers and lengths of bare branch in spring.	Bullfinches	21

Gooseberries, redcurrants and whitecurrants			
	Leaves stripped and skeletonized, large numbers of caterpillars present.	Gooseberry sawfly	36
		Magpie moth	36
	Leaves with irregular holes, especially young leaves.	Capsid bugs	21
	Shoot tips infested with tiny insects; leaves sticky, curled, distorted, sometimes blackened.	Aphids	20
	Buds pecked out in winter; poor blossom and bare lengths of branch in spring.	Bullfinches	21
	Tunnelling under tree; roots damaged.	Voles	23

Pears			
	Leaves and shoots infested with small grey, black or brown insects; leaves feel sticky and may be distorted.	Aphids	20
	Leaves speckled, bronzed or dried up; tiny insects on undersides.	Fruit tree red spider mite	37
	Young leaves in spring tattered and chewed; shiny beetles present.	Leaf weevils	27
	Leaves/shoots with blobs of white froth.	Froghoppers	35
	Young leaves, flowers and buds eaten; 'loopers' present.	Winter moth	38
	Leaves bound together tightly by threads; caterpillar inside.	Tortrix moth	38
	Leaf surfaces grazed by small, black, slug-like larvae.	Pear and cherry slugworm	39
	Leaves with yellow/brown blisters.	Leaf blister mite	39
	Fruitlets swollen and distorted, fall prematurely; small maggots inside.	Pear midge	39
	Fruits tunnelled; maggot inside.	Codling moth	37
	Fruits with irregular bumps and scars.	Capsid bugs	21
	Fruits pecked or chewed.	Birds	21
		Wasps	26
	Tunnelling under tree; roots damaged.	Voles	23

Plums and damsons			
	Leaves and shoots infested with green or green and yellow insects and sticky; leaves very tightly curled and distorted.	Aphids	20
	Leaves speckled, bronzed or dried up; tiny insects on undersides.	Fruit tree red spider mite	37
	Young leaves tattered in spring; shiny beetles present.	Leaf weevils	27
	Leaves with small ragged holes especially at shoot tips; fruits misshapen.	Capsid bugs	21
	Young leaves, flowers and buds eaten; 'loopers' present.	Winter moth	38
	Leaves bound together by threads.	Tortrix moth	38
	Fruitlets tunnelled, wet frass near entrance; fruitlets fall early.	Plum sawfly	39
	Fruits tunnelled; maggot inside.	Plum fruit moth	39
	Fruits pecked or chewed.	Birds	21
		Wasps	26
	Buds removed in winter; poor blossom and bare lengths of branch in winter.	Bullfinches	21
	Tunnelling under tree; roots damaged.	Voles	23

Strawberries			
	Underside of leaves covered in tiny pale-coloured insects; leaves sticky and possibly sooty.	Aphids	20
	Fruits partially or wholly eaten away.	Birds	21
		Wasps	26
		Snails and slugs	25
	Plants wilting; white or pale yellow larvae feeding on roots.	Wireworm	27
	Leaves yellowing and bronzing; minute mites on undersides.	Red spider mite	37

43

Organic pesticides

Safer sprays?

The sprays included here can be used in commercial organic production, according to the standards set by the Soil Association (SA) and the United Kingdom Register of Organic Food Standards (UKROFS). The Soil Association standards do, however, put them in a 'restricted' category, not for routine use. This is because they are not harmless. They may be less harmful and less persistent than many, but they are poisons and will, inevitably, harm creatures other than those we wish to kill. 'Organic' pesticides should be used with restraint, and should not be seen as an alternative to the many other organic methods that have been introduced in this book.

Effective spraying

All pesticides, whatever their nature, should be used correctly. This is essential both to ensure that they are effective, and also so that harm to the environment is minimized.

● **Do's**

Identify the problem first, then choose an appropriate spray.

Read the label and instructions carefully before opening the bottle.

Use a sprayer suitable for the job – one that is in good condition, gives a good even spray and does not leak.

Use the exact dilutions recommended and only make up the quantity of spray that you need.

Adjust the sprayer so that it gives good cover of the area being sprayed. Too coarse a spray will mean that a lot of the spray just runs off the plant; too fine a spray may result in the spray drifting on to other plants.

Spray in still weather to reduce spray drift.

Apply the spray to the relevant area. If a spray only works by direct contact with a pest there is no point in spraying parts of the plant that are not infested.

Store pesticides in their original packaging, in a secure, cool, dark place.

● **Don'ts**

Use a spray just because it is the only one you have at the time.

Use a spray against pests other than those for which it is recommended.

Add a little bit extra 'just in case' when diluting a pesticide.

Store made up pesticides.

Spray in windy weather.

Spray plants where bees are working.

Store pesticides in unmarked bottles and in places accessible to children.

Pesticides and bees

Pesticides are harmful to bees. To avoid killing or injuring these useful creatures, *never spray a crop where bees are working*. This means that when plants are in flower they should not be sprayed. If it is essential to spray, only do so in the evening when the bees have finished working. Alternatively spray on cool early mornings when the bees are less active.

If there are bee keepers in your neighbourhood, give them advance warning of any spraying.

'Organic' pesticides

Bacillus thuringiensis (Bt)
A bacterial disease of caterpillars.

Use against: caterpillars of the large and small white cabbage butterfly, cabbage moth, and the diamond back moth.

How it works: the pests must eat foliage which has been sprayed before they will be affected.

When and where: spray infested brassica plants, aiming to give a good cover of both sides of the leaves.

Cautions: Bt can harm a much wider range of caterpillars than those it is effective in controlling − but as it only harms those that eat it, it is relatively selective.

Derris
An insecticide made from the roots of plants of the Derris species. Available in liquid or powder form.

How it works: on direct contact with the pests; also acts as a stomach poison.

Use against: aphids, thrips, red spider mite, caterpillars, sawfly larvae, cane midge, flea beetle and raspberry beetle.

When and where: as Derris kills mainly on contact, and breaks down quickly after spraying, it should be applied directly on to relevant pests.

Cautions: Derris is poisonous to fish, so do not use near ponds or waterways. It is harmful to several beneficial creatures including adult ladybirds, some parasitic wasps and anthocorid bugs.

Pyrethrum
An insecticide made from the flowers of pyrethrum *Chrysanthemum cinerariaefolium*.

How it works: on direct contact with the pest.

Use against: aphids, small caterpillars and flea beetles.

When and where: as for Derris.

Cautions: one of the safest products to use near warm blooded livestocks; *poisonous* to fish. Harmful to some ladybirds. It is difficult to obtain pure pyrethrum; most brands have added piperonyl butoxide, which is not an acceptable organic spray.

Insecticidal soap
A mixture of potassium salt soaps of vegetable origin.

How it works: on direct contact with the pest.

Use against: aphids, whitefly, red spider mite, leafhoppers, pear and cherry slugworm, blackcurrant leaf midge, sawfly and soft scale.

When and where: Insecticidal soap has a contact action only, so the spray should be applied only directly to the pest, and infested parts of the plant. It can be used on crops up to the day of harvest.

Cautions: safe to people and pets, but can harm some beneficial creatures including ladybirds and their larvae. These soaps can damage sensitive plants (mainly in the greenhouse) so it is advisable to do a small 'spot test' before spraying the whole plant.

Soft soap
An old fashioned soap of vegetable origin.

How it works: on direct contact with the pest.

Use against: aphids. Soap is a mild insecticide which is often used as a 'wetter' to help other sprays stick to waxy leaves, e.g. plants of the cabbage family.

When and where: a contact killer, only harms those creatures that it actually touches.

Aluminium sulphate
This is only included for use against an epidemic of slugs. It is not truly 'organic'.

How it works: on contact with the pest, either direct, or as they move over it.

Use against: slugs and snails.

When and where: applied directly to the soil where slugs are a problem.

Cautions: avoid direct contact with young seedlings as it may scorch plants.

Spray chart

PEST	TYPE OF SPRAY	COMMENTS
Aphids	Soft soap or insecticidal soap	
Apple sawfly	Derris liquid	Timing is critical. Spray at petal fall. To avoid harming bees, spray at dusk.
Asparagus beetle	Derris liquid or dust	Apply to beetles and larvae.
Blackcurrant leaf midge	Insecticidal soap	Spray at first signs. Repeat after 3 or 4 days. Ensure spray penetrates curled leaves.
Brassica whitefly (see Whitefly)		
Caterpillars		Bacillus thuringiensis, Pyrethrum or Derris, spray or dust.
Cherry slugworm	Derris liquid or insecticidal soap	
Codling moth	Derris liquid	Best used in conjunction with traps. Spray 7–10 days after first moths are caught, repeating if necessary.
Flea beetle	Derris powder	Dust leaves.
Fruit tree red spider mite	Derris liquid or insecticidal soap	Derris also affects mites' natural predators.
Gooseberry sawfly & magpie moth	Derris liquid	If infestation is heavy, spray larvae whilst they are small.
Pea and bean weevils	Derris dust	Dust young plants.
Leaf weevils	Derris liquid or dust	Should not be used if blossoms are open.
Pea moth	Derris liquid	Spray a week after flowering. Repeat 2 weeks later.
Pea thrips	Insecticidal soap	
Pear slugworm (see Cherry slugworm)		
Raspberry beetle	Derris liquid or dust	At petal fall and when first pink fruit appears.
Raspberry cane midge	Derris liquid	Spray base of canes at the beginning of May. Repeat 2 weeks later.
Slugs and snails	Aluminium sulphate	Works on contact with pest. Use with caution (see page 45).
Whitefly (Brassica)	Insecticidal soap	Spray the undersides of leaves, perferably in the early morning when the pests are less active.
Winter moth	Derris liquid	Spray at bud burst.
Wasps	Derris dust	Puff into nest entrance at least an hour after sunset, when wasps are inactive.

Glossary

Brassicas: cabbages, Brussels sprouts, cauliflowers, kale, borecole, turnips, swedes, cress, salad, rape and mustards. All are closely related and are members of the 'Brassica' family of plants.

Cocoon: a silky or hard case made by an insect larva (e.g. caterpillar) to protect it while it is developing into an adult.

Frass: 'droppings' of caterpillars and other larvae.

Hibernate: to spend the winter in an inactive state.

Honeydew: sticky, sugary liquid produced by greenfly and other sap-sucking insects.

Larva (plural larvae): many insects go through several very different stages in their lives, starting as eggs which hatch out into larvae. These are often greedy feeding grubs, such as caterpillars and maggots. They bear no resemblance to the adult insects into which they will eventually develop. Caterpillars, for example, are the larvae of butterflies, moths and sawflies.

Legumes: peas, beans, clover and other related crops.

No-dig: a system of growing that avoids any turning over of the soil.

Overwinter: survive the winter.

Parasite: a creature or plant that lives in, or on, another creature or plant, and uses it as a source of food.

pH: a measure of the acidity of the soil. A pH of 7 is taken to be neutral; a soil with a pH of less than 7 is said to be acid, while a pH figure of more than 7 is said to be alkaline.

Pregermination: seed is allowed to germinate in a 'safe' environment, such as on wet kitchen paper in an airing cupboard, before it is sown.

Pupa: the stage of an insect between larva (*see above*) and adult. They are usually immobile and do not eat.

Resistant: a resistant variety is one that will suffer less from a particular pest than other varieties.

Sooty mould: a black, soot-like fungus that grows on honeydew (*see above*).

Virus: a microscopic organism that causes diseases in plants and animals.

Index   Chapter headings are in bold type.